W9-BWU-760

"Irwyn Ince is not merely a gifted thinker and writer on the subject of loving across the lines of difference. He is also, and has been for the duration of his life and ministry, a compelling practitioner of these important kingdom matters about which he writes. Irwyn is also my good friend. I have learned much from him and have been loved well by him. The same is true of the community that I serve, as we have drawn on Irwyn's wisdom in our own effort to honor the call of our Lord, who demolishes dividing walls and brings together Jew and Gentile—and every other race that is part of humanity—under Christ. If you are eager to move forward in the triune God's call to love and build community with those who are not like you, then this is the book for you."

Scott Sauls, pastor of Christ Presbyterian Church in Nashville, author of *Jesus Outside the Lines*

"In John 17 Jesus prayed that the church would be one, just as he and the Father are one. *The Beautiful Community* is a clarion call to the church to image our triune God in both our unity and diversity—to see and cherish the beauty of a diverse and unified body of Christ. The church needs this book more than ever, and I'm thankful Irwyn Ince has written it."

Christina Fox, writer, speaker, and author of *Closer Than a Sister: How Union with Christ Helps Friendships to Flourish*

"Irwyn Ince lays out a blueprint for the church in the twenty-first century. While we are individually made in the image of God, we are also corporately made in God's image as a body. At a time when we are as polarized and divided as ever, when culture is desperately trying to define our identity, there is no greater need than for God's church to model 'beautiful community' and true 'gracism.'"

David A. Anderson, author of *Gracism*, founder and senior pastor of Bridgeway Community Church in Columbia, Maryland

"Dr. Ince provides all Christians in the American context, and the churches in which they serve, an accessible and clear biblical and theological vision to help them work toward the unification of all things and all people in Christ. The book is grounded in a succinct and accessible biblical, theological, and historical vision for the 'beautiful community' and written with the prose of a concerned pastor who longs to see the people of God reach their redemptive potential in matters related to ethnic unity and racial conciliation. Readers might not agree with everything Ince says in this book, but they will certainly be challenged to consider carefully the biblical and theological imperative of pursuing what he calls the 'beautiful community.'"

Jarvis J. Williams, associate professor of New Testament interpretation at Southern Baptist Theological Seminary

"Irwyn Ince is a ministry-minded, biblically grounded Christian leader with equal passion for the unity and diversity of the body of Christ. In this historically informed, culturally relevant, and theologically astute book, Ince grounds his fresh vision for the beautiful people of God in the holy beauty of the triune God. I recommend this guide for anyone who is open to understanding the deeper reasons why racial reconciliation is essential to living out the gospel."

Philip Ryken, president of Wheaton College

THE BEAUTIFUL COMMUNITY

UNITY, DIVERSITY, AND THE CHURCH AT ITS BEST

IRWYN L. INCE JR.
FOREWORD BY TIMOTHY KELLER

An imprint of InterVarsity Press
Downers Grove, Illinois

InterVarsity Press
P.O. Box 1400, Downers Grove, IL 60515-1426
ivpress.com
email@ivpress.com

InterVarsity Press® is the book-publishing division of InterVarsity Christian Fellowship/USA®, a movement of students and faculty active on campus at hundreds of universities, colleges, and schools of nursing in the United States of America, and a member movement of the International Fellowship of Evangelical Students. For information about local and regional activities, visit intervarsity.org.

Scripture quotations, unless otherwise noted, are from The Holy Bible, English Standard Version, copyright © 2001 by Crossway Bibles, a division of Good News Publishers. Used by permission. All rights reserved.

While any stories in this book are true, some names and identifying information may have been changed to protect the privacy of individuals.

Cover design and image composite: David Fassett
Interior design: Jeanna Wiggins
Images: abstract watercolor: © Sergey Ryumin / Moment Collection / Getty Images
      blue green painted background: © enjoynz / iStock / Getty Images Plus
      Celtic trinity ornament: © ved007 / iStock / Getty Images Plus
      circle of dot pattern: © hudiemm / DigitalVision Vectors / Getty Images
      circular line pattern: © Serhii Brovko / iStock / Getty Images Plus
      orange painted background: © enjoynz / iStock / Getty Images Plus
      rotating line tunnel effect: © Vitan / DigitalVision Vectors / Getty Images

ISBN 978-0-8308-4831-7 (print)
ISBN 978-0-8308-5341-0 (digital)

Printed in the United States of America ♾

InterVarsity Press is committed to ecological stewardship and to the conservation of natural resources in all our operations. This book was printed using sustainably sourced paper.

Library of Congress Cataloging-in-Publication Data
A catalog record for this book is available from the Library of Congress.

P	19	18	17	16	15	14	13	12	11	10	9	8	7	6	5	4	
Y	35	34	33	32	31	30	29	28	27	26	25	24	23	22	21	20

"A sense of personal beauty comes,

I believe, only in the generous, self-giving gaze,

the noticing regard of another person."

ESTHER LIGHTCAP MEEK

FOR IRWYN L. E. INCE (1926–2009),

from whom I received a sense

of personal beauty before I knew what that was.

I never had to look for eyes to affirm my beauty and dignity

because his gaze always spoke a message of generosity,

selfless giving, and love matched only by

the actions that confirmed the message.

CONTENTS

FOREWORD

Timothy Keller

Nearly fifty years ago I enrolled at Gordon-Conwell Seminary. A small group of us single students, all of whom lived on campus, ate in the cafeteria three times a day and became something of an informal theological dinner club. Several of my most life-shaping friendships emerged from this group. The most significant one, of course, was my friendship with Kathy, my future wife.

But another was Elward Ellis, an African American student who went on to be a leader with InterVarsity Christian Fellowship and a Presbyterian minister. One day Kathy and I were with Elward and we said something about race that he corrected gently. We responded that we were indeed ignorant in this area and would be happy to listen to him. I remember that there was a twinkle in his eye when he said, "Really? Are you really asking me to be truthful with you about the subject of race? Will you be willing to be instructed by me?"

We may have swallowed hard when we said yes because we wondered if we were going to be scolded. But that's not what Elward did. Over the next couple of years, Elward simply paid us the compliment of speaking with candor. He laid out some basic ideas about race and race relations that we never forgot. I remember three particularly vividly.

One was that white folks did not have to be personally bigoted toward individuals of another race in order to support social, educational, judicial, and economic systems and customs that automatically privileged whites over others. This is more often recognized now, but at the time it was a completely new idea to us. Like most Americans, we thought that every person's condition was purely the result of their own choices, so that if you were poor it was mainly your fault. Elward showed us that this was simplistic to the point of being false.

Another was that the Euro-white culture is nearly invisible to white Christians. "When you come to my church," he said, "and you see how we worship and sing and preach, you think 'that's the black way.' But when you look at your own church you just think 'that's the right way.'" He went on to explain that white Christians don't realize how much of what they say and do in church is not from the Bible but rather is shaped by cultural factors. As Irwyn says in this book, these are cultural "preferences," not biblical principles, but white Christians tend to absolutize them in our minds. By making our cultural preferences normative for everyone, we not-so-subtly invite white people to come to our churches while inviting non-white people to stay away.

A third thing we learned was why white people are so unaware of these realities. Elward said, "We [non-whites] have to know the white culture in order to survive. When we come into your workplaces and retail spaces and organizations, we have to learn how you regard time and use space, how you understand relationships between the individual and the group, how you think and solve problems, and express emotion and handle failures and judge status. But for you to function well in your society, you don't need to understand us or our culture and differences." In short, nearly every racial minority in the US understands Euro-white culture pretty well, but we whites are far more ignorant of how the cultures of others operate.

That means that in mixed race churches, the burden of relationship maintenance tends to fall disproportionately on racial minorities, even if they are well represented statistically. Elward once said to us, "You can pick up the topic of race for an evening discussion and then the rest of your week you don't need to think about it. Race is an abstraction for you—something 'out there'. For me—every time I look in the mirror I think of race. We have to think about it all the time, but when we get into a church with white brothers and sisters and want to talk about it as much as we need to, you all quickly get tired of it."

These things and others that Elward told us have helped us enormously to understand race and so much of what goes on in the church. We'd never heard anything like them, and it was decades before we began to see them in print. Today there are more places for white evangelicals to hear and consider them—and one of the best places is here in this book by Irwyn Ince.

Irwyn lays a solid theological foundation for the idea that the multiracial church is God's will. He begins by looking at the doctrine of the Trinity itself, then expounds the judgment at Babel, its reversal at Pentecost, the growth of the multiracial churches in the book of Acts, and the final destination—the church of "every tongue, tribe, people, and nation" in Revelation 7.

In particular, he examines how our Christian identity gives the basis for multiethnic fellowship. Biblical scholar Larry Hurtado described how the uniquely "translocal and transethnic" identity of being "in Christ" created the first multiethnic religion in history, because Christian conversion relativizes our cultural and social identities without effacing them. Irwyn backs up this claim extensively and shows how both individual and group identity formation bear on the development of racially and culturally diverse Christian churches and ministries.

After the doctrinal groundwork, Irwyn lucidly and candidly lays out so many of the dynamics of which Elward spoke to us long ago.

He draws on recent scholarship to show how much racial exclusion is structural—rather than all due to personal, conscious racial animosity—and is therefore hidden from whites. He makes visible the cultural preferences and ethnic identities that feel so primordial and absolute.

Finally, this book provides a host of practical ways for a church to live out Paul's exhortation to a church of diverse ethnicities to "accept one another . . . just as Christ accepted you, in order to bring praise to God" (Romans 15:7 NIV). These include diversifying leadership so each ethnic group is truly co-owner and co-creator of the community. It means listening to one another about musical expressions in worship. It means leaders especially learning intercultural skills, and all the church's members developing significant crossracial friendships. And that is just the start.

I recognize in Irwyn's book so much of the wisdom, honesty, and compassion—the speaking truth in love—that Kathy and I received through our first significant crossracial friendship. May this volume spark and inspire the forging of thousands of such relationships across our church and country. Few things are more needed.

Timothy Keller
Founding Pastor
Redeemer Presbyterian Church, New York

INTRODUCTION

I **was an excited boy** in the summer of 1978. Not only was I a few weeks away from my tenth birthday (double digits finally!), but my parents, grandparents, sister, and I were about to go to Disney World. Who wouldn't have been excited? That trip was full of memorable moments—riding Space Mountain with my dad and sister, seeing all the Disney characters live and in color, and, of course, the Florida weather.

The indelible mark that Orlando trip left on me was made in the hotel pool, not at the amusement park. My sister and I were playing with our inflatable float when another boy came over and asked to play with us. We were more than happy to have someone else join in on the fun. He wanted to try out my float. No problem. Our parents taught us to be willing to share our toys. He had a different kind of float than mine, so I asked him if I could play with his float. His response was, "No, because you're colored."

Maybe this is surprising, but I had never heard the phrase "You're colored" in my life.

We lived in Brooklyn, New York, part of the melting pot that was New York City. It's not as though I didn't recognize racial difference. A few of the adults at my school were Indian, including the principal who didn't assimilate to Western culture in her manner of dress. Her clothing style

> *From that moment in the pool on, I became racially awake.*

remained the same as it would have been if she were living in India. I had a diverse group of friends in school and in my neighborhood. So, although I saw color, I never had a derogatory or pejorative personal encounter of difference.

From that moment in the pool on, I became racially awake.

I knew that what he said was wrong, but I didn't know why he said it. I remember being sad at the situation rather than mad at the boy. When I told my mother about it later in the day, she said, "Someone taught him that. There's nothing wrong with you." When I returned to school and we reported on what we did over the summer, I told my teacher about the incident. My Indian-American teacher said, "Well he doesn't know that he's colored too. White is also a color."

You see, all of this—my interaction with the boy in the pool, my mother's response, my teacher's retort—speaks to the definitive reality that to live in the United States of America is to navigate through racial differences, racial divides, and racial hostilities. It has been, to use Ibram Kendi's words, "Stamped from the beginning" of our nation's history. At some point in your life, whether you are born and raised in America, or have immigrated here from another country, race and racism will meet you in relationships and institutions.

RACIALLY AWAKE AND AWAKE IN CHRIST

In my life, this reality worked itself out into a rejection of the Christian faith during my late teen years and an embrace of a Black nationalistic worldview during my college years. For a few years of my life, practically every thought and activity was in some way motivated by or centered on this worldview. I attended protest marches, led book studies at school, and helped to provide security for some of the leaders of the Afrocentric movement. My rejection of Christianity was active. It was the white man's religion. So, I immersed myself in books to help shape an Afrocentric worldview: *African Origins of Major*

Western Religions and *Africa: Mother of Western Civilization,* by Yosef A.A. ben-Jochannan.

Dr. Molefi Asante put the idea of Afrocentricity forward in two books published in the late 1980s, *The Afrocentric Idea* and *Afrocentricity*. I agreed with Asante that Christianity, as well as Islam, was contradictory to "Diasporan Afrocentricity." Christianity makes us submit to a strange God. So, even though the Black Church in America had historically been the "single most authoritative force" in the Black community, Christianity was not ideal for people of African descent.

The ironic perspective of this position was the Black Church actually needed to eventually distance itself from Christianity. It needed to realize that it was "among our most authentic contact with the gods of our ancestors, not the strange God of Christianity." And its authentic contact to African religious expression made the Black Church "the most logical institution for the beginning work of instructing the masses concerning African customs, habits, and styles." The Black Church will then be an agent through which Afrocentricity will "rise on the *sanctification* and *deification* of our history as a way to save ourselves."

I was in lockstep with the Afrocentric movement's views and never saw myself returning to an embrace of the Christian faith. However, in the good providence of God, I at least believed that the Black church had a role to play in the Afrocentric resurrection of African Americans. This made me willing to attend a Black church in Washington when my wife and I moved from Brooklyn and settled just outside of DC.

As we began to attend church regularly and immerse ourselves in a weekly young adult Bible study, the Spirit of God chipped away at my heart of stone. God's Word came alive to me. What I once rejected with hostility I now received with gladness.

> *God is the one who writes our life's story of faith in Jesus Christ.*

God is the one who writes our life's story of faith in Jesus Christ. It is often the case that his Spirit uses this story to ignite a ministry passion in us. People who God delivers from addiction become passionate about seeing and helping others know that same deliverance. The ones he brings out of a life of sexual sin want to testify to others about God's power to free them from the same. Those who know freedom in Christ from the idolatry of trying to make a great name for themselves delight in seeing others experience that freedom for themselves. What I am saying is that the Lord often uses our life story to create in us a divine dissatisfaction with the way things are.

DIVINE DISSATISFACTION

In the concluding words of his Southern Christian Leadership Convention address in 1967, Dr. Martin Luther King Jr. exhorted his hearers with the challenge to depart with a divine dissatisfaction. That is, a God given dissatisfaction with the way things are when contrasted with how they ought to be according to God's standard.

God exposes his heart to us in his Word. He declares his purposes for his creation. Yet the effects of human sin permeate the cosmos. Things are not the way they ought to be. It is impossible to be a Christian and not have a divine dissatisfaction with particular ways in which the reality of sin impacts us, our neighbors, our institutions, and our world.

A divine dissatisfaction involves me, but it starts with God. In God's kingdom, what has the curse undone that he is committed to restore and make right? It would take too long for us to list what God has committed to restore from what sin's curse has undone. Yet, there are certain points of dissonance that will strike the chords of our hearts because of our respective stories.

For me, this dissonance is the overwhelming mono-ethnicity of most churches in the USA. The fracture, polarization, and ghettoization of humanity that began when Adam and Eve delighted in a created thing more than they delighted in God still presses in on the church today. The root of this ghettoization is fully displayed in the Tower of Babel account in Genesis 11 where disunity became the norm. This is so significant that we will spend a full chapter examining the fracture at Babel later in the book.

The Lord has promised to renew all of creation. We will enter the time of no more—no more death, no more tears, no more pain—in his timing. And when we do, there will be no more polarization.

My divine dissatisfaction is with the historic and contemporary complicity of the church in the racial and ethnic polarization of our congregations. My divine dissatisfaction is over our apparent contentment with this status quo.

God graciously rejected my rejection of him. His love for me burst into my consciousness at an historic Black church in DC. Yet, my divine dissatisfaction also began there. As I read the Scriptures, I began to realize how much I had made my ethnic identity an idol. I began to see that, from the beginning, God stamped his commitment to reverse the ghettoization of humanity and make a kingdom from every tribe and language and people and nation. This multiethnic, crosscultural, diverse kingdom of people will one day reign on the earth (Revelation 5:9-10).

In Ephesians 1:10, the apostle Paul helps us understand that God's plan of salvation is much more magnificent than individual people confessing and repenting of their sins and believing in Jesus Christ. That is surely magnificent, but the glorious gospel is God's plan to unite everything in Jesus Christ, both things in heaven and things on earth. Every rupture in the cosmos will be repaired. This is where we are headed—the reign and rule of Jesus Christ over everything and everyone. If the church is anything, it is a real-time, tangible expression of this future reality. Peter Leithart says it well:

The good news is the good news of the unity of the human race. And the Church is a proleptic sign of that eschatological reality. It is a sign of the unity of the human race that will one day be perfectly achieved. It is also a sign of a cosmic unity that all things are summed up in Christ, and the Church is to be the visible communion of human beings that anticipates that ultimate union of all things in Christ. It is a living sign; a community where that unity is already experienced in some degree. . . . This, in some respects, is the whole point of redemptive history. That God is going to knit back the human race in his Son. *When the Church fails to be that proleptic reality of the eschatological union of all things in Christ, then we are very deeply failing in the calling we've been given.* (emphasis added)

Years ago, one of my seminary professors gave us a description in class of the kingdom of God that made me pause. I needed to hear it again. "Would you repeat that?" I asked. He did. "To [Jesus] the kingdom exists there, where not merely God is supreme, for that is true at all times and under all circumstances, but where God supernaturally carries through his supremacy against all opposing powers and brings man to the willing recognition of the same."

Where God carries through his supremacy against the forces that oppose it and brings people to the willing recognition of that supremacy, we get a glimpse of God's kingdom. In this regard, the church is a manifestation of his supernatural power and kingdom purposes. The church is a living sign of the union of all things in Christ because he supernaturally reconciles us to God and to one another by the power of his Spirit. Refusing to pursue this reconciliation is akin to resisting the heart of God. It means failing the calling we have been given as the people of God.

Peter Leithart's quote refers to the church as a whole, the universal church. However, we participate in the visible communion of the church through our membership in a local congregation. Thus, the ministry of reconciliation is primarily pursued and demonstrated in the context of a local church. My divine dissatisfaction, codified more positively as a core conviction, is this:

The ministry of reconciliation demonstrated in the local church by the gathering of people from diverse backgrounds, cultures, and ethnicities is the natural outworking of a rich biblical commitment.

I have just described what I call beautiful community.

BEAUTIFUL COMMUNITY

This book is about beauty more than anything else. Beauty that is created and recreated by God.

Scripture is rich with illustrations of God's attributes.

The Lord is good.	The Lord is just.
The Lord is love.	The Lord is holy.
The Lord is mighty.	The Lord is a banner.
The Lord is peace.	The Lord is a shield.
The Lord is a provider.	The Lord is majestic.
The Lord is a healer.	The Lord is a stronghold.
The Lord is merciful.	The Lord is near.
The Lord is gracious.	The Lord is a helper.
The Lord is kind.	The Lord is faithful.
The Lord is a refuge.	The Lord is all these things
The Lord is great.	and more!
The Lord is righteous.	

I began each of those sentences with "The Lord is" instead of "God is" to emphasize a point. We know these attributes as people who have been supernaturally brought into a covenant relationship with him, as people who call him Lord. "We should think about God's attributes as servants, within the covenant relationship," writes John Frame. In other words, as Christians, our understanding of God and our experience of him is not a theoretical declaration that fails to touch the fabric of our lives. No. We come to know these things about him, because we belong to him. So, let me rephrase my core conviction with a subtle change.

The ministry of reconciliation demonstrated in the local church by the gathering of people from diverse backgrounds, cultures, and ethnicities is the natural outworking of a rich covenantal theological commitment.

As people of the covenant, we pursue beautiful community. We do it because our Lord is beautiful. The Lord's beauty may not be the first attribute that comes to mind when we think of him, but I want to promote its place among the lavish list of attributes that delight our hearts. His beauty is instructive for how we think about what it means to be his people.

Dutch Reformed theologian Herman Bavinck helps us when he says, "The pinnacle of beauty, the beauty toward which all creatures point, is God. He is supreme being, supreme truth, supreme goodness, and also the apex of unchanging beauty."

In the pages that follow, we will discover how God's beauty is seen in his trinitarian life. He is the apex of unchanging beauty as Father, Son, and Holy Spirit in eternally existent, mutually glorifying, loving, honoring, and supporting diverse community. The Father, the Son, and the Spirit are distinct persons, yet they are one God. Bavinck again says, "The Trinity reveals God to us as the fullness of being, the true life, eternal beauty. In God, too, there is unity in diversity, diversity in unity."

When God declares in Genesis 1:26, "Let us make man in our image, after our likeness," he is deciding to make us in his image not only as individuals. We are his image as a mutually loving, honoring, and supporting diverse community. We glorify him in this. And we are beautiful.

The question is what will enable us to commit to the pursuit of beautiful community—unity in diversity—seeking the unity of the Spirit across lines of difference? What will enable us to actively resist the pernicious polarization that has been present in the church in America from the beginning? It will not be the fact that diversity is a hot topic in culture today. It will not be the pressure to appear viable or acceptable to the world. The pursuit is too hard. It is too perplexing, and often too painful, if our commitment is not drenched in the beautiful truth that we are participating in the beautiful plan and purpose of our beautiful God.

PART 1

SEEING AND KNOWING OUR BEAUTIFUL CREATOR

THE HOLY AND BEAUTIFUL HABITATION

Our Relational God

> *Look down from heaven and see,*
> *from your holy and beautiful habitation.*
>
> ISAIAH 63:15

S hortly after joining All Saints Church, Joyce was asked to serve on a Mercy and Justice ministry board for the city. At first glance, it sounded like a good development. She was a new member, there was a ministry need at the church, and the leadership asked her to serve in a leadership position right away. But what began with positive intentions quickly became offensive to Joyce.

She explained that being Black and growing up in a predominately white neighborhood enabled her to understand the dynamics of being a minority in a majority setting. Even still she initially felt unable to connect deeply with the non-Black members of All Saints Church. When she was asked to serve on the board, she said it made her feel the way she felt as a child—something she had never been able to articulate. She described this experience as making her feel as somewhat of a token.

"I was immediately asked to be on the board. And some people might be like, 'Oh, that's really great.' But they didn't know me. They didn't know my character. They don't know who I am. They just know that I'm Black and I'm a female." Joyce explained that the church's leadership viewed her as a good fit to serve on the board because of her master's level education. "I felt like I was chosen to participate in something that is really important for reasons that do not show you who I am as a person."

In other words, she felt as though she was valued more for the role she could play than for who she was as a human being. Joyce wanted to be known, not commodified. This is a shared human desire, wanting to be known. As Charles Taylor writes, "The very way we walk, move, gesture, speak is shaped from the earliest moments by our awareness that we appear before others, that we stand in public space, and that this space is potentially one of respect or contempt, of pride or shame." We know that we appear before others and, therefore, we have an innate desire to be known by those before whom we appear in a way that communicates respect. And we need that respect to be on our terms, not solely on terms imposed upon us by others.

This is the case with human relationships, but, amazingly, the God of all creation wants to be known as well. Consider our sinfulness, our imperfections, and the ways we hide those shortcomings from others. It ought to boggle our minds that the perfect and holy God who sees everything wants to be known by us. Not in a creaturely way, as though he would lack something if he remained unknown. Rather, he wants us to know him for our delight. Joyce realized that the leadership at All Saints required more than information about her—she's Black, she's a woman, she's married, she has a master's degree—to truly know her. So it is with God. To know God is not simply to possess facts about him. We know God as those who stand before him, as we submit to him. We are in fellowship with the living God as he teaches us about both himself and ourselves. Esther Lightcap Meek notes well that "it is not the knower who is in the driver's seat, but rather the yet-to-be-discovered reality." God is in the driver's seat when it comes to making himself known to us.

What made Joyce feel like a token was the lack of relationship. It wasn't a fact or information problem; it was an intimacy problem. In other words, knowing is covenantal. Knowing God as those who stand before him, who submit to him, and who are in fellowship with him is to say that we know him as our covenant Lord. For God to be in the driver's seat means that he sets the conditions and standards of our relationship with him. Because he is in control, we don't get to tokenize him. "Rather than taking him for granted, as we do with impersonal things and forces, we must always take his concerns into account, responding to him in repentance, love, thanksgiving, worship." Of course, the problem is that we do not always take God's concerns into account. We do not always respond to him in repentance, love, thanksgiving, and worship. We regularly take God for granted through unbelief and willful ignoring of his concerns.

> *To know God is not simply to possess facts about him. We know God as those who stand before him, as we submit to him.*

Joyce's dilemma is actually an apt description of the human problem concerning God. The heart of humanity's problem is the one described in Genesis 3—a loss of intimate relationship with God and one another. In the Garden of Eden, nothing hindered our vertical or horizontal relationships. Indeed, the last verse of Genesis 2 is a portrait of intimacy: "And the man and his wife were both naked and were not ashamed" (2:25). Everything was exposed to everyone. Every aspect of the relationship between God and humanity shone in the light. And it was beautiful. Try to grasp the magnitude of the moment when sin entered the picture. Humanity's first impulse was to hide from the presence of the Lord God (Genesis 3:8). Biblical scholars have rightly pointed out that the death sin brought into the world was threefold. It was physical; we became subject to decay. It was judicial; we lost our innocence and became guilty before God. And it was spiritual; we lost intimacy and fellowship with God. We have been trying to hide ever since. But God was not and is not content to let us continue deceiving ourselves into thinking that our efforts at camouflage actually work. A central facet of the Bible is God's desire and commitment for us to know him as Lord.

A FELLOWSHIP OF KNOWING

In Isaiah 63:15 the prophet requests that the Lord look down from his holy and beautiful habitation and see his people's condition. He confesses, "You are our Father," while lamenting, "Abraham does not know us, and Israel does not acknowledge us" (v. 16). The people have strayed far from the faith of their fathers, so much so that their fathers would neither recognize nor acknowledge them. Yet Isaiah's plea relies not on being acknowledged by their fathers, but on the fact that he knows God as Father. You see, God has disclosed himself and this is a gift. It has always been a gift and as fallen creatures, our knowing God is a gift of his grace.

God's dwelling, heaven, is envisioned as a holy and beautiful habitation. The imagery of a beautiful or glorious habitation indicates knowing God as Lord requires a covenant relationship with him. Who are those who know that God's dwelling place is a holy and beautiful house? Those whom God has graciously brought out of darkness and into his marvelous light that they might see his beauty. Alec Motyer describes this verse as being addressed to the Lord in the fulness of his divine nature: "The prayer is addressed to the Lord in the fulness of the divine nature, his transcendence (*heaven*), dignity ('house'), 'holiness' and beautiful or winsome glory."

God's divine nature connects intimately to real life. What is your vision of God? Do you envision radiance, glory, and beauty? God brings us into relationship with him so that we will know him as our glorious Lord who dwells in beauty. We do not have time for a thorough biblical exploration of that wonderful truth in this work, but we will take a brief look at a few key texts to help us see it, beginning with God's famous address to the people of Israel.

Signed, Sealed, Delivered. "And God spoke all these words, saying, 'I am the LORD your God, who brought you out of the land of Egypt, out of the house of slavery. You shall have no other gods before me'" (Exodus 20:1-3).

These words form the preamble to the constitution of the newly formed nation of Israel and the first of the Ten Commandments. It is basically saying to them "Signed, sealed, delivered, you're mine." This is so that their life in response to God will be "Signed, sealed, delivered, we're yours."

In the preamble God identifies himself by name: Yahweh, the Lord. He had previously identified himself by name to Moses back in Exodus 3:14 at the burning bush. Now he directly reveals himself by name in the hearing of the people. However, what we ought to find striking about this self-identification is how personal it is. He does not simply say, "I am the Lord God." He declares, "I am the Lord, *your* God." The assembly of people gathered at Mount Sinai have something the other nations do not have. God identifies himself with his people. If any of us is able to say to God, "Signed, sealed, delivered, I'm yours," it is only because God has said it of us first. Professor and theologian John Frame remarks, "This expression in effect makes Israel part of God's own name. Yahweh is 'Yahweh thy God,' Yahweh the God of Israel. How remarkable it is that the Lord of glory so profoundly identifies himself with his sinful people!"

Who has earned the right for God to speak to them with such a term of relational intimacy? The answer is no one. What is more, no one is able to claim this relational intimacy *with* God apart *from* God declaring it. In other words, there's a difference between knowing that there is a God and knowing God. Knowing God always includes loving fellowship initiated by him toward us. It is sheer grace. There is a day coming when the whole earth will be full of this kind of knowledge of the Lord (Isaiah 11:9; Habakkuk 2:14).

> *In other words, there's a difference between knowing that there is a God and knowing God. Knowing God always includes loving fellowship initiated by him toward us. It is sheer grace.*

Knowing the Lord. Our second passage picks up the promise of loving, intimate fellowship with God and moves it further along.

> Behold, the days are coming, declares the LORD, when I will make a new covenant with the house of Israel and the house of Judah, not like the covenant that I made with their fathers on the day when I took them by the hand to bring them out of the land of Egypt, my covenant that they broke, though I was their husband, declares the LORD. For this is the covenant that I will make with the house of Israel after those days, declares the LORD: I will put my law within them, and I will write it on their hearts. And I will be their God, and they shall be my people. And no longer shall each one teach his neighbor and each his brother, saying, 'Know the LORD,' for they shall all know me, from the least of them to the greatest, declares the LORD. For I will forgive their iniquity, and I will remember their sin no more. (Jeremiah 31:31-34)

In Joshua 24 we find Joshua leading the people of Israel in a covenant renewal ceremony. The Lord had fulfilled his promise to deliver them from slavery in Egypt and bring them into a land flowing with milk and honey. Of all the good things that the Lord promised, not one of them had failed (Joshua 23:14). As we saw in the preamble to the Ten Commandments, the Lord's usual pattern is to demonstrate his love for us through his saving power then call his people to obedience. Now that the people have arrived in the Promised Land, their covenant relationship is renewed. After laying out all that the Lord had done for them, Joshua clearly states the issue: "Choose this day whom you will serve. If it is the gods who your fathers served at the edge of the river, or if it is the gods of the Amorites whose land you are dwelling in. But as for me and my house, we will serve the Lord" (Joshua 24:15, author's translation). The people respond emphatically. "Far be it from us that we should abandon the Lord to serve other gods. . . . We also, we will serve the Lord, for he is our God" (24:16, 18b, author's translation). Joshua then tells them about the problem with their affirmation. "You will not be able to serve the Lord because he is a holy God. He is a jealous God. He will not forgive your transgressions and your sins. For you will forsake the Lord and you will serve gods of foreigners. And he will turn, and he will treat you badly, and he will consume you. After that he will do good to you" (24:19-20, author's translation).

Joshua's prediction came to pass. The people turned out to be covenant breakers instead of covenant keepers. By the time we reach Jeremiah's day, the consequences of the peoples' rejection of their Lord had begun coming to fruition. This rips at Jeremiah's heart, bringing him to tears (Jeremiah 9:1-3). He is the prophet appointed by the Lord to usher the nation of Judah into exile. The Lord sent him to root up, tear down, destroy, and devastate. Then, to build and plant (1:10).

Jeremiah 31:31-40 is at the heart of the Lord's plan to build and to plant. It is the promise of a new covenant, a better one (Hebrews 8:6). Of course, the problem with the old covenant lay not with the Lord, but with the people (Hebrews 8:8-12). Their leaders did not know the Lord (Jeremiah 2:8). Since loving fellowship with God, or lack thereof, has ethical implications for how we live, Jeremiah characterizes the nation's lack of knowing God by their greed for unjust gain (6:13). There is an intimate connection between their behavior and their knowledge of God, specifically as it relates to their violating the Ten Commandments. Jeremiah stands at the entrance to the temple and asks, "Will you steal, murder, commit adultery, swear falsely, make offerings to Baal, and go after other gods that you have not known, and then come and stand before me in this house, which is called by my name, and say, 'We are delivered!'—only to go on doing all these abominations?" (Jeremiah 7:9-10). The list of accusations directly names the first, second, sixth, seventh, eighth, and ninth commandments. Note that violating the first commandment, "You shall have no other gods before me," happened when they chased after other gods they *have not known*. They rejected the God that they knew by seeking to know other gods in the same way.

Therefore, it's no surprise when we discover the crux of the new covenant is, "They shall all know me, from the least of them to the greatest, declares the LORD" (Jeremiah 31:34). From the least of them to the greatest has a dual emphasis. It promises a fellowship of knowing with the living God from the youngest child to the oldest adult and it envisions people from both ends of the social structure loving and serving the Lord from their hearts. We may even say that this is a vision of the eternal life that Jesus gives. "And this is eternal life, that they know you [Father], the only true God, and Jesus Christ whom you have sent" (John 17:3). To know the Lord is life and glory.

United to Christ. "For what we proclaim is not ourselves, but Jesus Christ as Lord, with ourselves as your servants for Jesus' sake. For God, who said, 'Let light shine out of darkness,' has shone in our hearts to give the light of the knowledge of the glory of God in the face of Jesus Christ" (2 Corinthians 4:5-6).

The culmination of our fellowship of knowing with the living God is found in our being united by faith to Jesus Christ. The same voice that said, "Let there be light" (Genesis 1:3) radiates the beauty of his holy habitation into the center of our being so that the intimacy with God that we so desperately need becomes ours through Jesus Christ. From the beginning, God has specialized in bringing light into darkness. The darkness of our sinful condition is overcome by the effulgent glory of God in Jesus Christ. His is the face, as Esther Lightcap Meek says, that will not go away.

PERSONAL, COLLECTIVE, COMMUNAL KNOWING

Jesus Christ is the answer to Isaiah's request for the Lord to look down and see from his holy habitation. Divine beauty has broken in on us through him. We are enabled to pursue the fellowship of knowing with our neighbors by the glory of God in the face of Jesus Christ, the beautiful countenance that will never turn away from us. The fellowship of knowing God is personal, collective, and communal.

This is how it was for Joyce. She struggled with feeling like a token at All Saints, commodified because she fit a desired profile for their ministry board. They did not know much about her, which caused her to recognize that there was not a lot of authenticity happening at her church—a perception that began to change for Joyce three years into her membership at a women's retreat. Prior to the retreat she did not feel as though she could connect with the women in the room. She attended the retreat feeling depressed and disappointed about personal issues that she described as having nothing to do with the people in the room. Some non-Black women who she felt were particularly opened up to her and their vulnerability caused the guards and barriers in her heart to come down. She experienced

> *Jesus Christ is the answer to Isaiah's request for the Lord to look down and see from his holy habitation.*

these women as sisters in Christ and began to feel a real sense of connection. Following the retreat, she began to believe that people in the church who invited her family over for dinner were not just doing so out of a sense of Christian duty. They were being authentic. She said, "It became more real." In other words, what developed for her was a personal and communal fellowship of knowing. Her relationships at All Saints church began to reflect the relationship we have with God as we are brought into communion with him.

2

THE BEAUTY OF THE LORD

Our God Is Beautiful Community

> One thing have I asked of the LORD, that will I seek after:
> that I may dwell in the house of the LORD all the days of my life,
> to gaze upon the beauty of the LORD and to inquire in his temple.

PSALM 27:4

Performance-enhancing drugs are a major problem in the sporting world. Cycling, baseball, weightlifting, football—athletes at the highest levels need something to put them over the top or keep them in the game. Usually, Botox doesn't make the list of PEDs. But that was the precise drug that prompted twelve disqualifications at an event in Saudi Arabia. A dozen camels were disqualified from a camel beauty contest in January 2018. Their crime? Doping in the form of Botox injections. The purpose? So that they would appear more beautiful in the eyes of the judges.

Of course, the camels didn't inject themselves. A veterinarian obviously hired by the camels' owners performed the plastic surgery. The doctor was caught just days before the beauty contest. In fact, the attempt to enhance the camels' physical beauty wasn't limited to the injections. Since smaller, delicate ears are also a standard of camel beauty, surgery was performed on their ears. You're unlikely to ever come across a camel beauty pageant in America, but we know what it's like to commodify beauty, to parade people across a stage and judge the value of their physical appearance.

This prompts an important question: What is beauty? To have any kind of beauty pageant is to assume that we know what beauty is. Up to this point, I've talked about beauty extensively but have not defined it. Maybe we intrinsically know what beauty is. When we see someone or something appealing to our eyes, we say that person or thing is beautiful. When we hear a musical composition that resonates with us, we call it beautiful. What do we mean by that?

In the first chapter, we focused on our need to know God and to be known by him in a fellowship of knowing. He dwells in a holy and beautiful habitation. Who is this God that we need to know as Lord? There are many ways to talk about him, but I want to put this simple declaration before you. The Lord is beautiful. Beauty is an attribute of God, but one through which we are able to view the majesty of all his other perfections.

The truth is we only know beauty in relation to the one who is inherently beauty. All beauty in the world is derived beauty. All beauty has as its source the beautiful one, God himself. Jonathan King rightly says, "The existence of beautiful things requires, if you will, the existence of a Beautifier." Indeed, God is the source of everything that is not God. Whatever beauty we create, no matter how surprising, is always reliant on there being something else—the material we work with. That material, including our imagination, has its source in God.

PERFECTION, PROPORTION, AND PLEASURE

In the thirteenth century, Thomas Aquinas codified beauty as being directly connected to Jesus Christ with three characteristic features.

He wrote, "Species or beauty has a likeness to the property of the Son. For beauty includes three conditions, *integrity* or *perfection*, since those things which are impaired are by the very fact ugly; due *proportion* or *harmony*; and lastly, *brightness*, or *clarity*, whence things are called beautiful which have a bright color."

Steven Guthrie helpfully distills Aquinas's definition into three *P*'s: Perfection, Proportion, and Pleasure. To speak of perfection as an aspect of beauty in relation to God and his kingdom is actually mysterious. The perfect diamond is flawless. Makeup is able to cover over blemishes on the face of a news anchor. Photographs can be photoshopped to remove the imperfections of an image. But the perfection of our Lord's beauty "is not the airbrushed sheen of the fashion magazine." His perfection of beauty has room for scars.

The marks of human history—human sinfulness, depravity, and injustice—are indelibly inscribed upon the flesh of the resurrected Lord, carried into the life of the new creation by the Spirit, and transfigured. These marks in no way tarnish the glory of the new creation, but rather "those wounds, yet visible above" are "in beauty glorified."

My wife and I have four children, three boys and a girl. Three of them are grown and the fourth is not far behind. Though I am decades removed from the day of each one's birth, the memory of those moments still shines brightly in my mind. When my wife and I held each newborn child, warmly wrapping them in our arms, lovingly gazing upon this brand-new person, our conviction was simple: "He's perfect." "She's perfect." Each child was unique, but perfect in our eyes. It's not as though we believed that the son or daughter we cradled in our arms would be error free or lack any flaws. Yet perfection was an apt word to describe what we were experiencing in that moment because our child was exactly who God intended him or her to be.

The mystery of perfection as an aspect of beauty is its transcendence. It points to a glory beyond itself. I knew that when I held my children, I didn't simply cradle flesh and blood. I held a living soul who had not existed before the moment of conception and who would exist from that point into eternity. This perfection also includes hope that just as the wounds of the crucified, risen, and ascended Savior are in beauty glorified, the life he gives will speak a perfecting redemptive word over the wounds and flaws we all endure.

To say that proportion is an aspect of beauty is to say that harmony matters.

Proverbs 25:11 says, "A word fitly spoken is like apples of gold in a setting of silver." A word given at the right time in the right way, suitable for the occasion, is beautiful. To say that proportion is an aspect of beauty is to say that harmony matters. The Bible speaks to us about peace a great deal. The Hebrew word, *shalom*, translated into English as "peace," means more than simply the absence of strife. It is the presence of well-being, wholeness, harmony, the world fitting and functioning together as it ought. When we talk about proportion as an aspect of beauty, we are talking about shalom. So it's important to note that this harmony does not refer to uniformity. To talk about proportion is to talk about the relationship between things. Where the mystery of perfection is in its ability to accommodate scars, the mystery of proportion is the presence of unity in diversity. "When all things are what they are in all their glittering variety, and when all of these are joined together in a cosmos—in a universe—it is beautiful."

In one respect, the beauty of proportion is the story of Scripture. Genesis 1 recounts the Lord bringing order out of chaos. The world was without form and darkness stretched over the surface of the deep (Genesis 1:2). This description of creation's chaotic formlessness resolves as God forms and fills the earth in the six days of creation. Days one, two, and three are paralleled by days four, five, and six. The light (form) created on the first day is filled with the sun as the greater light to rule the day and the moon as the lesser light to rule the night. The expanse of day two that forms the sky and the seas is filled with the birds and fish on the fifth day. The dry land and vegetation are formed on the third day and filled with land animals and human beings on day six. There is a benediction, a blessing declared over each day with the words, "And God saw that it was good." Six times we hear this refrain. Then God makes humanity, the crown of his creation, and bestows a blessing upon them (v. 28). After looking at everything he has made, he declares his creation "very good" (v. 31). Each day is good because the formlessness of chaos further dissipates. We get the highest good on the sixth day because all is well and properly ordered. Chaos and disharmony are no more. Beauty says with profound clarity, "All will be well." Genesis 1 sets the trajectory for humanity's call to image God in bringing order out of chaos as well as his commitment to restore shalom throughout creation after sin destroys harmony in Genesis 3.

Just as it is with perfection, proportion is transcendent and points us forward in hope to glory. God will make all things beautiful in their time (Ecclesiastes 3:11). We long for well-ordered lives. We long for harmony in our communities and in our relationships. We long for peace in the world. How many songs have been written about humanity's longings for harmony and peace? This is a longing for beauty, for all things to be the way they ought to be.

The third note of the triplet in the rhythm of beauty is pleasure. Church father Saint Augustine describes its coupling by saying, "If I were to ask first whether things are beautiful because they give pleasure, or give pleasure because they are beautiful, I have no doubt that I will be given the answer that they give pleasure because they are beautiful."

Beauty causes us to delight when we experience it. Jonathan King refers to beauty's ability to evoke pleasure or delight as a unique characteristic of beauty. The mystery in perfection and proportion appears in pleasure as well. This facet of beauty is also seen in the benedictions at the end of each day of creation. Pleasure and delight are included in the words, "It was good." That is, the goodness of each day was about more than its usefulness for God's purposes. Goodness wasn't simply about utility. What God created was good because it brought pleasure. In the mini-Sabbaths at the end of each creation day, God didn't work. Rather, he delighted over the goodness of what he had created.

When we think of delight, we typically do so in the sense of what we personally enjoy. Delight, then, becomes solely subjective. It is only in the eye of the beholder. However, the mystery of beauty's pleasure is that it is a de-centered delight in another. While I experience pleasure (or *we* experience it in community), my wants are not at the center of that experience. This delight is not self-centered. Guthrie writes, "Rather than drawing the beautiful object into the orbit of my concerns, I am the one drawn in." The beautiful doesn't serve my (our) interest. It captures it. There is a magnetism, if you will, to beauty.

Oh, how true this is of God! He is beautiful and we are captured by his beauty. The weight of his presence, his glory, is captivating. King David declares as much in Psalm 27:4:

> One thing have I asked of the LORD,
>> that will I seek after:
> that I may dwell in the house of the LORD
>> all the days of my life,
> to gaze upon the beauty of the LORD
>> and to inquire in his temple.

The Hebrew word that practically every English translation of the Bible renders as "beauty" includes the sense of pleasantness or delight. David is speaking words of affection for the Lord. He is captivated by the thought of having his gaze fixed upon the Lord. The vision is one that is pleasing but not because David wants to experience something that makes him feel good. It's a delightful vision because he is gazing upon his light and salvation, the one who is the strength of his life (Psalm 27:1). The delight is in the Lord, not in himself.

SIMPLICITY

The facets of beauty—perfection, proportion, and pleasure—give us a lens through which to understand my declaration, "The Lord is beautiful." There is, however, one more feature of beauty that deserves attention. It is not a fourth facet, but a strand that runs through the three *P*'s—simplicity.

Simplicity is a hot topic these days. Experts tell us that simplifying our lives is a key to better health and longevity of life. They instruct us to declutter everything from our homes to our relationships and our minds. Get rid of the excess and you will increase in happiness, they say. The simple living gurus may be on to something. We feel the tension and disorientation of having too much going on.

My son, Nabil, is a gifted musician, songwriter, composer, and hip-hop artist who goes by the stage name "Seaux Chill." One of the joys of parenting is when your children begin to teach you. During Nabil's sophomore year in college, he released a music project with nine original songs titled *I Heard God Laughing*. The first song, "The Beloved's Intro," begins with a poem about beauty, simplicity, and love.

> The sky tonight has a certain elegance to her.
> The second great light has provided a unique kind of brightness.
> One through which seems to have God intentionally reaching
> out to his lovers.
> As I look up, clouds suspended in perfect bliss part,
> and the light appears to have centered on me.
> The beauty of God's masterpiece had me paralyzed.
> It's almost as if the beloved was saying,
> Stop and look. There was so much beauty to be found in

simplicity.

I thought for a moment and replied,

My dear Friend, as always, you are right.

There is enough beauty in this one night to keep me infatuated
until I meet you face to face.

I could feel God crack a smile.

For a while longer I pondered.

Then I proceeded to ask,

Why can't life be this beautiful?

Why can't life be this simple?

He simply responded,

Nabil, never cease to drown yourself in my love.

"Stop and look. There was so much beauty to be found in simplicity . . . Why can't life be this beautiful? Why can't life be this simple?" He has put his finger on the pulse of the tension. We want simplicity and we inherently know that beauty exists. For example, a software programmer finds delight in an elegantly developed code. Its elegance lies in achieving the same program result with less lines of code. Nothing unnecessary is included. It fits well together and brings order to a problem. Indeed, in the simply elegant software code we find the facets of beauty—perfection, proportion, and pleasure.

While we would love for this simplicity to mark our lives, we don't really know how to get it or keep it. But when we turn our gaze to the beauty of the Lord, we find that simplicity is fundamental to his nature. "None of his attributes can be removed from him, and no new attribute can be added to him." God has no excess baggage. He needs no decluttering.

The Lord's simplicity is powerfully demonstrated in this foundational creed: "Hear, O Israel: The LORD our God, the LORD is one. You shall love the LORD your God with all your heart and with all your soul and with all your might" (Deuteronomy 6:4-5). This creed is called the Shema, which is a transliteration of the Hebrew imperative meaning "hear" or "obey." What did the Lord command his people to obey? First that he is "one." What does it mean to obey that the Lord is one? It certainly includes a commitment to monotheism. There is only one God and, therefore, his people are to have only one Lord whom they worship. But it is more than that. The Shema speaks to the simplicity of God. He is undivided. He is not fragmented. Professor Scott Redd describes it well writing, "God's character is whole, pure, full, rich, and simple." But for us, "The most obvious image of humanity's shattered simplicity is the scene of Adam and Eve—the images of God—hiding behind the hedge when their Lord calls them in the cool of the day. Fragmentation must be maintained by careful secrecy and deceit." Dr. Redd has keyed in on the fact that our desire for beauty in simplicity is frustrated by our fragmentation. This fragmentation is internal and external, individual and corporate, public and private. It is another way of understanding the death pictured in Genesis 3 that I described in chapter one. We will take time to explore this further in the chapters to come. For now, it is enough to note the difference between us and the Lord.

The Lord our God is one—beautiful unity, simple perfection, proportion, and pleasure.

BEAUTY AND SIMPLICITY IN THE TRINITY

The Lord is beautiful. The one who dwells in a holy and beautiful habitation wants to be known by us. So he reveals himself to us as the Lord who is one, unity in diversity as Father, Son, and Holy Spirit. The mystery of beauty in perfection, proportion, and pleasure is due to the source of beauty. "The testimony throughout Scripture is that God is one. At the same time, without contradiction, the Scriptures present the mystery of three persons who are God: Father, Son and Holy Spirit." Fragmentation, division, disharmony, and disunity are our story, but they are not God's. His is the story of beauty and it is most profoundly seen in his communal life.

That God is Trinity is a mystery so deep it will never cease to inspire awe. How can it be that there is one God who exists in three eternally distinct persons? I don't know. Such knowledge is too high for me. What I do know is that this is who the Bible declares God to be. Volumes and volumes have been written on the nature of our triune God over the course of Christian history. Here, we're focused on beauty and the particular beautiful community that is God.

When the Lord Jesus Christ was baptized Scripture tells us, "Immediately he went up from the water, and behold, the heavens were opened to him, and he saw the Spirit of God descending like a dove and coming to rest on him; and behold, a voice from heaven said, 'This is my beloved Son, with whom I am well pleased'" (Matthew 3:16-17). The Father delights in the Son's obedience. The Spirit anoints him for his messianic ministry. Father, Son, and Spirit affirm one another, declaring by word and action that they are united in plan and purpose. The Father's affirmation is important because the Son will appear as though he is outside of the Father's will when he is forsaken by his friends and by his Father (Matthew 26:31; 27:46). The Spirit's anointing is necessary because the Son needed to faithfully endure temptation to save humanity from its sinful, fragmented life of rebelling against God (Matthew 4:1).

> *Far from a dry, secondary, unimportant technical doctrine, God as Trinity—unity in diversity, diversity in unity—is the heartbeat of the Christian faith.*

We also find out that, in addition to being united in saving his people, the triune God sustains them through suffering. The apostle Peter puts it this way: "Peter, an apostle of Jesus Christ, To those who are elect exiles of the Dispersion in Pontus, Galatia, Cappadocia, Asia, and Bithynia, according to the foreknowledge of God the Father, in the sanctification of the Spirit, for obedience to Jesus Christ and for sprinkling with his blood: May grace and peace be multiplied to you" (1 Peter 1:1-2). Peter is writing to Christians and he refers to them as "elect exiles." They live as people who are longing for a true and permanent home as they endure suffering for belonging to Jesus. Peter will tell them that their faith is being tested and that they should not be surprised by the fiery trial that has come upon them (1:7; 4:12). But he begins his letter with the reminder that their triune God is for them. Peter describes them as elect exiles according to the foreknowledge of God the Father, which is a covenantal declaration. Knowing is covenantal. Through his foreknowledge, the Father has bound himself to his people in love. Part of the evidence for this is the sanctification of the Spirit. The Spirit is at work in, among, and through them for a purpose—a life of obedience to Jesus Christ. In other words, they cannot lose because all of God is for them!

Far from a dry, secondary, unimportant technical doctrine, God as Trinity—unity in diversity, diversity in unity—is the heartbeat of the Christian faith. The Father, Son, and Holy Spirit are perfectly united in beautiful community. Theologian Herman Bavinck says well, "The Trinity reveals God to us as the fullness of being, the true life, *eternal beauty*" (emphasis added).

Years ago, Rodney King was brutally and tragically beaten by Los Angeles police officers. The city exploded in riots for six days after three of the four police officers, each of whom were white, were acquitted in a jury trial. Famously, King called for an end to the violence in a 1992 interview. "Can't we all just get along?" he asked. These words are inscribed on his tombstone. It is a question that continues to dog humanity as our fragmentation continues to remain on display. But it's not a question the triune God has ever needed to ask of himself. In our search for peace and unity, what is our example? What is our aim? How will we actually know when peace has been achieved?

John Lennon asked us to imagine a day when all the people would share all the world and the world would live as one. A world without greed, hunger, or murder is also a world without concern for heaven, hell, or religion—without God. We cannot fully imagine what unity among diversity looks like apart from a vision for the beautiful life rooted in God's essence. Nor can we fully live in the hope that unity is humanity's destiny. To really imagine such a future, we have to know God as he has revealed himself to be! We have to have been brought into the inner life of God, as those who share in that life through faith in Jesus Christ. "The Trinity belongs to the inner life of God, and can be known only by those who share in that life." We experience a vision of beautiful community as we experience the inner life of God.

This beautiful inner life of God was described by ancient church fathers with the term *perichoresis*. The term itself takes us beyond utility to beauty because it describes a divine dance. Technically, it is the concept that the three persons indwell and interpenetrate each other. The Father, Son, and Holy Spirit each fully and mutually fill and are filled by one another as each is an embodiment of the same ineffable substance. In other words, they are joined together in a beautiful, eternal, and inseparable dance. We hear a derivative of the Greek word *perichoresis* in our English word *choreography*.

I used to love watching the show *So You Think You Can Dance*. I would gaze in utter delight at the abilities of young women and men to move their bodies with incredible rhythm and grace, even when the music was sharp and dancing to it demanded rough edges. The solo performances were remarkable, but the choreographed partner performances rose to another level. The nearly flawless partner dances sent a chill down my spine. Yet at the end of the performance, when the music stopped and they hit their final pose, the joy on their faces came with heaving chests. In those few moments before the judges, they gave everything they had and were left gasping for breath. They could not continue to dance that way forever. The dance had to end because fatigue and the necessities of life demanded it. But with God, the flawless dance has no beginning and it has no end! John Frame explains it this way:

> The concurrence of the three persons of the Trinity in all that they do is a profound indication of their unity. There is no conflict in the Trinity. The three persons are perfectly agreed on what they should do and how their plan should be executed. They support one another, assist one another, and promote one another's purposes. This intra-Trinitarian "deference," this "disposability" of each to the others, may be called "mutual glorification."

To say that the Lord is beautiful is to say that he is beautiful community. His beautiful, simple love is expressed in perfect agreement between Father, Son, and Spirit. It is expressed in the way the Son defers to the Father (John 4:34; 5:30; 6:38-39). We see it in the way the Father supports the Son (Matthew 3:17; 17:5). We experience it in the way the Spirit proceeds from the Father and is sent by the Son (John 15:26; 16:7). God is the apex of unchanging beauty as Father, Son, and Holy Spirit in eternally existent, mutually glorifying, loving, honoring, and supporting diverse community—a never-ending, beautifully choreographed divine dance.

3

THE PERFECTION OF BEAUTY

Knowing Ourselves

The Mighty One, God the LORD, speaks and summons the earth
from the rising of the sun to its setting. Out of Zion,
the perfection of beauty, God shines forth.

PSALM 50:1-2

Andrew appreciates the fact that his church, Cross Community, had church-wide conversations around issues of discrimination, social justice, and police brutality. He tried to listen to his brothers and sisters in Christ and step into their shoes, but that alone was not enough. As a white young man, he inherited a keen awareness of how differently we experienced life following a pickup basketball game. Here's how he described the experience of one of the Black men in the group:

> We were playing basketball, then we were going over to a restaurant. On the way . . . I looked over and he was pulled over. The police were searching his car. I realized that afterwards. I wondered, *Should I turn around? Should I try to get in the middle*

of that? So, I was just praying for him. He got to the restaurant eventually and he was just distraught. He was just depressed about it. Like, "I can't believe they treated me like that. I can't believe they were saying some of those things to me and accusing me of stuff I wasn't doing."

He compared his friend's experience to his own teenage years when he should have been arrested on a number of occasions only to have the police let him go. It was a stark realization for him of how ethnic identity plays a significant role in the experiences people have with law enforcement even today. Apart from his friendship with this young Black man, he may have only ever known this truth at an arm's length, as a concept rather than a felt reality. The dignity divide has yet to be healed.

BEAUTY AND DIGNITY

In its opening message, the Bible declares that human beings are made in the image of God, after his likeness (Genesis 1:26-27). What does this declaration of image mean? In one sense, it's about beauty. I love how Elaine Scarry describes beauty's influence: "Beauty brings copies of itself into being. It makes us draw it, take photographs of it, or describe it to other people." She's speaking here about beautiful objects, but I envision the overflow of God's beauty in the creation of humanity. God, the beautiful one, brought copies of himself into being. He did not need to make us. We didn't come into being because God lacked someone with whom to share his love or because he needed our worship. No, there was, and is, no lack in God. He is fully complete in his internal life of mutual glorification and love as Father, Son, and Holy Spirit. We come from the overflow of God's beauty and love. Therefore, as someone recently said to me, things are more beautiful than they need to be. We are unique among creation. Every person, from the womb to the tomb, has a beauty and a value independent of our abilities or what we produce. Simply put, if I said to my wife, "I don't find you beautiful, but I do find you useful," I wouldn't be married very long. And rightly so!

Every person, from the womb to the tomb, has a beauty and a value independent of our abilities or what we produce.

God established this personal beauty. Richard Pratt points out that Genesis 1:26 establishes humanity's unique place in God's kingdom. God has given the human race the unique title of image-bearer. Pratt goes so far as to ask his readers to put down his book, go find another person, and shake his or her hand while saying with sincerity, "Hello, your Majesty!" What this means is that individual human beings possess inherent beauty, dignity, and worth since each one has been created in the image of God. This is, in fact, a royal dignity imprinted on every person across race, ethnicity, class, education, age, ability, and gender. Consider Nonna Verna Harrison's comments on Genesis 1:26:

> The word "dominion" speaks of royalty, which is a facet of the divine image in every human person. Royalty involves (1) dignity and splendor, and (2) a legitimate sovereignty rooted in one's very being. . . . Because everyone is made in the image of God, and because this image defines what it means to be human, people are fundamentally equal, regardless of the differences in wealth, education, and social status. The church preached this counter-cultural message in the ancient world and still preaches it now.

The countercultural message that the church preached in the ancient world was that all people are fundamentally equal due to their being bearers of the divine image. It was the ancient message and should also be the modern message of the church today.

Genesis was penned first for the people of Israel who had been set free from slavery in Egypt. In the ancient Near Eastern world, the *imago Dei* was a radically countercultural idea. The nations of that time recognized only one who imaged or embodied the gods and that was the king. This image was not borne by the common person walking the street and it certainly wasn't attributed to a woman. Dignity, value, and worth were ascribed to persons through their association with the king. Were they one of his people? Were they a citizen? Did he view them favorably? These were the qualifying questions. It is no surprise, then, that noncitizens and foreigners could be oppressed or enslaved without any thought given to whether or not doing so was an immoral act.

Egypt relegated the people of Israel to slavery simply because they were not Egyptian. The first chapter of Exodus tells us that a new king arose over Egypt who did not know Joseph (Exodus 1:8). The people of Israel had existed for generations in Egypt following Joseph's elevation to prime minister and the migration of Jacob and his descendants from the land of Canaan. As the Lord promised, they had grown from a nomadic band of seventy to a swarming multitude of people (Exodus 1:7). Seeing a growing nation filling the land within his own nation caused the new pharaoh to say, "Behold, the people of Israel are too many and too mighty for us. Come, let us deal shrewdly with them, lest they multiply, and, if war breaks out, they join our enemies and fight against us and escape from the land" (Exodus 1:9-10).

If I were to put Pharaoh's speech into the current American vernacular, he says, "We've got a problem with these immigrants." Pharaoh, in these verses, delivers the Egyptian State of the Union address. The citizens are assembled to hear him say, "We have a major national crisis. These people are different than we are and we've let them practically take over our country. They're stronger than us!" Creating fear among people in order to gain their support is not a new political tactic. Pharaoh played on the Egyptian's sense of ethnic and national superiority, which is on display back in Genesis 43. As second in command in Egypt, Joseph would have looked like an Egyptian and spoken the language. His brothers, for the second time, had come down from Canaan to buy grain. Joseph prepared a banquet for them, but he sat at his own table. In verse 32 of that chapter we're told that the servants served Joseph by himself and then they served the brothers by themselves. The Egyptians who ate with Joseph were also separate from the Hebrews because Egyptians could not eat with Hebrews, as it was considered an abomination within Egyptian culture.

That attitude hasn't changed by the opening chapter of Exodus. Pharaoh doesn't have to create a sense of national superiority. He just has to use it for his advantage. If we were to place Exodus 1:10 in a modern context, he says, "People of Egypt, we've got to deal shrewdly with these immigrants. We've got to be wise in how we deal with the Hebrew problem. They are a threat to national security. We have a whole nation of non-Egyptians living in our country. They're not loyal to us and if war comes, they'll join with our enemies and fight against us. They'll take your jobs. They'll take your wealth. They'll take your property. They'll take your power!" I invite you to see the parallels, to listen to the bells that go off in your minds. We can look at that text and see the evil at work in Pharaoh's heart. We can clearly see the power of hell behind the problem presented in the text. But we should be able to make the connection to our current day as well.

You might feel deeply about the ways in which we talk about immigration in America. Every presidential candidate in this generation has to discuss their proposals for the "immigration problem," as if the topic does not include real people made in the image of God who are deserving of dignity. The US Census Bureau predicts that by 2044 America will become a "majority minority" population. And some folks have a problem with that.

Here's my point: wherever we encounter a *those people* attitude in America's current immigration debate, we witness a heart that is closer to Pharaoh than it is to Jesus Christ. Pharaoh's words in Exodus 1:9-10 ought to remind us that the *imago Dei* imprinted on every soul has implications for how we think about and treat all people. In Egypt, Pharaoh was considered the only image of God. So if you weren't "his people" you could be dismissed as unworthy of dignity. We have a natural tendency to categorize people into groups of "others." Doing so makes it easy to dehumanize people and think of them only as a commodity. God would not have us look at image bearers in that way!

God liberated his people from bondage in Egypt. Then, through Moses, he gave them the book of Genesis. Thus, the ancient story of Genesis 1 is delivered to a newly liberated people. God essentially communicates to them, "The first thing I want you to understand about humanity is that everyone is an image-bearer!" The Hebrews were not to look like the cultures around them, placing value on people according to their usefulness. We see this principle woven throughout the first five books of the Old Testament, particularly in the fourth commandment:

> Observe the Sabbath day, to keep it holy, as the LORD your God commanded you. Six days you shall labor and do all your work, but the seventh day is a Sabbath to the LORD your God. On it you shall not do any work, you or your son or your daughter or your male servant or your female servant, or your ox or your donkey or any of your livestock, or the sojourner who is within your gates, that your male servant and your female servant may rest as well as you. You shall remember that you were a slave in the land of Egypt, and the LORD your God brought you out from there with a mighty hand and an outstretched arm. Therefore the LORD your God commanded you to keep the Sabbath day. (Deuteronomy 5:12-15)

No one is to work on the Sabbath day. The law applies not only to family members, but to their servants as well as the sojourner. Notice that rest and refreshment aren't the sole prerogative of the privileged people of Israel. When the Sabbath day comes, what are they to remember? They are commanded to recall their enslavement and their liberation made possible by the mighty hand and outstretched arm of their Lord. Egypt denied the dignity they were due, an act not to be replicated among God's people.

The inherent dignity of humanity is part of the reason God forbids idolatry, the practice of giving our worship and devotion to creation. So the second commandment is also of particular relevance to the issue of human dignity.

> You shall not make for yourself a carved image, or any likeness of anything that is in heaven above, or that is in the earth beneath, or that is in the water under the earth. You shall not bow down to them or serve them, for I the LORD your God am a jealous God, visiting the iniquity of the fathers on the children to the third and the fourth generation of those who hate me, but showing steadfast love to thousands of those who love me and keep my commandments. (Exodus 20:4-6)

John Frame points out that respect for God's true image is included in the grounds for this second commandment. We learn that God is not only concerned about his dignity, he's concerned for ours. In the commandment he elevates and protects human dignity by forbidding the worship of images. He has already declared humanity to be his image in the world. Therefore, idolatry is a dehumanizing act, an act wherein we discard our own dignity. To worship an idol is an insult to God, ourselves and our neighbors.

G. K. Beale makes a similar point in reference to the language of imagery and idolatry in the book of Isaiah. He notes that the prophet

Isaiah makes an intentional contrast between the nation of Israel being crafted by God and Israel crafting their idols. The emphatic point is that God is the only one who has the authority to establish his authentic image. The creation should look at humanity and see a reflection of God's glory. Therefore, worshiping idols is an affront to human dignity because it prevents people from reflecting God's glory as we ought. God created us to reflect his glory and his beauty to the world. The second commandment reminds us that just as God is not content to remain unknown, neither is he content to leave us to our dignity-denying idolatry. The Lord knows that the unavoidable outworking of idolatry is oppression and injustice. He gave us the second commandment to protect and prevent us from this tragedy.

IDENTITY AND DIGNITY

The issues of individual dignity are intimately tied to identity, which begs two important questions: who are we and how do we know? Ingrained in our being is the desire for a self-identification that accords with dignity.

In 2018 actor Sterling K. Brown won the Golden Globe for best TV actor for his role in the show *This Is Us*. During his acceptance speech he thanked producer Dan Fogelman at length saying,

> Throughout the majority of my career I've benefitted from colorblind casting. Which means, "Hey, let's throw a brother in that role." It's always really cool. But Dan, you wrote a role for a Black man. That could only be played by a Black man. And what I appreciate so much about this thing is that I'm being seen for who I am. And being appreciated for who I am. And that makes it that much more difficult to dismiss me. Or to dismiss anyone who looks like me.

Do you hear his delight as he thanks his producer for affirming his dignity? Colorblind casting occurs when filmmakers realize they need some diversity in the cast. So they look for a person of color to fill a role, thereby avoiding an all-white or homogenous cast. For example, I recall seeing *Star Wars* in the movie theater several times in 1977. Even though I was only nine years old, I also remember some of the public backlash around the fact that not a single Black person was featured in the film. James Earl Jones famously voiced Darth Vader, but viewers never saw his face, or any Black face for that matter. Did the writers and producers imagine a galaxy far, far away that lacked Black people? When *The Empire Strikes Back* released three years later, Billy Dee Williams suddenly appeared in a prominent role! Colorblind casting. While Sterling Brown may have benefitted from colorblind casting, it still meant that his identity as a Black man could be easily dismissed. What a marked difference it makes to know a creator had you on their mind from the beginning of a project and not as an afterthought.

Brown's speech was a vulnerable moment because although individual dignity is an ontological truth, we do not live as isolated individuals. We live in community and we need the truth to be affirmed. In his book, *The Soul of Shame,* Dr. Curt Thompson is spot-on when he says, "We are all born into this world looking for someone who is looking for us, and we remain in this mode of searching for the rest of our lives." That is to say we do not create ourselves out of thin air. There is no such thing as an affirmation-free existence. From the moment we open our eyes, we're looking for someone who is looking for us. Thus, what is central to us often comes from what matters to others. Whether we like it or not, there is a connection between receiving affirmation from others and embracing our dignity as image-bearers. This actually runs counter to the way we typically think about individual dignity.

In his book *Sources of the Self: The Making of the Modern Identity*, Charles Taylor writes that an individual's dignity consists of many facets, but commonly includes a sense of power, a sense of dominating public space, any invulnerability to power, and any self-sufficiency. We like to pursue a sense of dignity that isolates us from having to need external affirmation. Why are the superheroes we create in comic books and movies super? Typically, they have power beyond normal human capacity. They dominate a public space when they exercise their power. They have some measure of invulnerability (armor, shield, speed, etc.). And they are often loners. People depend on them, but they resist the need to depend on others. Even the way we fantasize about what it means to be super reveals what we generally believe about identity and dignity.

I believe that Taylor is right in his assertion that the absence of a self-identification that includes dignity can be catastrophic because it undermines one's sense of self-worth. This is why it is so important to root individual dignity in the *imago Dei*. It is also why our greatest need in life is to know God as Lord. Richard Pratt, following John Calvin, claims that without knowing of God, people

What is central to us often comes from what matters to others.

are unable to know themselves. Thus, a lack of knowledge of God results in people being confused about who they are. This confusion has a cost. Failing to realize the unique role that God has given people in his kingdom results in vacillating between self-degradation and self-importance. Pastor and theologian R. C. Sproul, seeking to clarify personal identity from a Christian perspective, explains that annihilation of personal identity or loss of self is not the goal. "The goal is a heightened understanding of the self as it relates to God. It is the redemption of the personal identity, not the destruction of it." Professor Steve Guthrie asks, "How do we know our identity or that of others around us? . . . I understand who I am by recounting a particular story to myself—a history that gathers together and plots all the disparate events of my experience." This story is written by the Spirit of God.

The Christian view of the self looks back to the goodness of God's original design and looks forward to the renewal of all things in Christ. Thus, woven into self-identification is God-given royal dignity where we place our story rightly into God's story.

ANCIENT AND MODERN TIMES

Nonna Verna Harrison argues that this message of royal dignity as the image of God has been church's countercultural message since the ancient world. Without question, the words of Genesis 1:27 identifying male and female humans as the image of God was a countercultural message in the ancient world. This countercultural message that human worth was not limited to one gender gets expanded to nations and ethnicities in passages like Isaiah 49:5-6 where it takes on a sharpened focus in the announcement of the good news in Jesus Christ. Included in this good news is the acceptance of ethnic, gender, and socioeconomic division. The reality of union with Jesus Christ manifested itself in his people striving for unity with one another across ethnic, gender, and socioeconomic lines. Yes, the message is ancient, but it is still as necessary to proclaim as ever.

On July 4, 1965, Rev. Dr. Martin Luther King Jr. preached a sermon at Ebenezer Baptist Church in Atlanta, Georgia, titled "The American Dream." He said,

> The whole concept of the *imago Dei*, . . . is the idea that all men have something within them that God injected. Not that they have substantial unity with God, but that every man has a capacity to have fellowship with God. And this gives him a uniqueness, it gives him worth, it gives him dignity. And we must never forget this as a nation: there are no gradations in the image of God. Every man from a treble white to a bass black is significant on God's keyboard, precisely because every man is made in the image of God. One day we will learn that. We will

know one day that God made us to live together as brothers and to respect the dignity and worth of every man.

Dr. King was talking about America, the reality of racism, and the shameful truth about life in a racialized society. Three years after this sermon, Dr. King was assassinated in Memphis, Tennessee, where he had travelled after two African American men, Echol Cole and Robert Walker, were killed when the electrical switch on their sanitation truck malfunctioned. The compactor turned on and crushed them to death. But the story was not that simple due to the long and pervasive arm of racism in the city. In spite of a torrential downpour on February 1, 1968 that caused the streets and sewers to flood, the sanitation workers were required to work. Cole and Walker were among the all-Black male sanitation workers working in those horrid conditions. After their deaths, Memphis public works refused to compensate their families. Eleven days after their deaths, as many as 1,300 black sanitation workers in Memphis walked off the job, protesting horrible working conditions, abuse, racism and discrimination by the city, according to the King Institute at Stanford University.

The motto for the strike did not come from Dr. King, but from Rev. James Lawson. On February 24, 1968, at Clayborn Temple in Memphis, Rev. Lawson included these words in his sermon, "For at the heart of racism is the idea that a man is not a man, that a person is not a person. You are human beings. You are men. You deserve dignity." When the protestors proceeded out of the doors of Clayborn Temple, they carried signs with four simple, yet profound words: "I Am a Man." The dignity divide was on display in full measure. These African American men had to say, "This city, this country, will not recognize or promote our dignity as human beings. So we will shout it out loud!" Such is the nature of humanity. We know inherently that we are image bearers, and that this comes with an ontological truth—we are endowed with incomparable dignity. Idolatry results in the denial of dignity, one that cannot be suppressed indefinitely.

And still, there is another aspect to this story, relating to dignity and the church. Today, if you stand across the street from Clayborn Temple and look at its façade, you will find these words engraved in the stone edifice above the large stained-glass window:

We know inherently that we are image-bearers, and that this comes with an ontological truth—we are endowed with incomparable dignity.

SECOND PRESBYTERIAN CHURCH
ORGANIZED, 1844

In the late 1940s, Second Presbyterian moved eastward from its inner-city Memphis location. In 1949 the African Methodist Episcopal (AME) church purchased the building and re-named it Clayborn Temple. Even this story, then, includes the reality of a racialized society having an impact on the church. A white church relocates, leaving its brown neighbors to maintain a more comfortable and homogenous life. Today, the "I Am a Man" Plaza stands outside of Clayborn Temple as a part of the "Clayborn Reborn" project. Second Presbyterian church of Memphis remains a majority white church, but one actively pursuing repentance and reconciliation—seeking to build bridges and love its neighbors well, especially across racial lines.

We are no longer in 1965. Progress has been made, but the work is not done. We are far from close to being able to loudly proclaim and promote the immeasurable dignity of every human being. As long as sin abounds idolatry will abound. And as long as idolatry abounds, the dignity-denying tragedy of injustice and oppression will abound. We could argue that too much of the church's role in the history of America rejected the countercultural message of the *imago Dei* and we have a lot of catching up to do as the people of God in living out its implications.

A CROWN OF BEAUTY IN THE HAND OF THE LORD

Beautiful Community as God's Image

> *You shall be a crown of beauty in the hand of the LORD,*
> *and a royal diadem in the hand of your God.*
>
> ISAIAH 62:3

I n her 2015 TED Talk, journalist Afua Hirsch recalls an encounter with a former coworker who expressed his reasons for excitement upon learning she was pursuing a new career in journalism. He said, "You're a woman. . . . You have great ideas. You're young." But the man became visibly nervous and looked away awkwardly before adding,

> "And you're . . . you're Black." I couldn't help but laugh. I tried not to let him see me laughing at that. And I wondered why is it so awkward for him to say something to me that is so obvious? . . . There are various reasons why this happens. And it happens all the time. And I think on one hand, he was unsure of whether that

was an insulting thing to say. And on the other hand, maybe he was unsure as to whether that was how I see myself.

Hirsch describes identity as a crucial aspect of humanity with which people grapple. Questions arise from encounters like this: "Who am I?" "How do other people see me?" "How do I see myself?" Whether or not people ask these direct questions, they demand attention because people's differences are implicitly or explicitly evident.

Our differences are no accident. Even if people prefer sameness, "God apparently loves difference; he created so much of it," says Duane Elmer. These abundant human differences become a source of difficulty when people are forced to navigate them in the context of relationships with others. Immediately after describing her interaction with her former colleague, Hirsch illustrates how the contrasting ways people perceive their differences cause identity challenges. This time, Hirsch, her boyfriend, and his young nephew were dining at a restaurant. In the context of a playful joke, her boyfriend pointed out that they were the only three Black people in the restaurant. The nephew responds, "There're not three Black people! There're two Black people. She's white!" Hirsch, brown-skinned and from a different region of London, did not fit the image the young boy had in his mind of a Black person. The same woman is identified as Black in one setting and white in another.

If identity were independent of external influences and simply a matter of personal conviction, this conundrum may not be worth discussion. However, we are made in and for community and our understanding of ourselves is intimately tied to our relationship with others. Dr. Brené Brown says, "Connection is why we're here. We are hardwired to connect with others, it is what gives purpose and meaning to our lives, and without it there is suffering." To put it another way, "We are born out of, in, and for community, and we cannot for a moment exist apart from it." The first facet we discussed of the *imago Dei* was the immeasurable dignity, value, and worth it places upon each person regardless of race, ethnicity, class, gender, or age. From there we explored the way idolatry leads to dignity-denying sins like oppression and injustice. Now it's time to introduce the second facet: for humanity to be the image of God, it must embody beautiful community—unity in diversity, diversity in unity. If God displays his beauty in his trinitarian life, we should expect that beauty to be reflected in the humanity that images him. While each person is royalty, we find the fullest expression of the image in community.

Therefore, both the dazzling diversity of humanity and our need for community are a fundamental aspect of the image of God. God is the apex of unchanging beauty as Father, Son, and Holy Spirit in eternally existent, mutually glorifying, loving, honoring, and supporting diverse community. As his people, when we are mutually glorifying, speaking, and acting in ways that enhance the reputations of one another, striving to bring praise and honor to others, exhibiting a mutual deference, a willingness to serve one another, and submit to one another— especially across lines of difference—we are imaging God's beauty.

> *If God displays his beauty in his trinitarian life, we should expect that beauty to be reflected in the humanity that images him.*

THE IMAGE: BEAUTIFUL COMMUNITY

As I mentioned in the introduction to this book, my passion to see the church pursue beautiful community was sparked when I realized that my racialized worldview was out of accord with the gospel. I had placed my racial and ethnic identity at the center of my identity (more on that issue later). As the hymn writer Charles Wesley wrote, "Thine eye diffused a quick'ning ray. I woke, the dungeon flamed with light. My chains fell off, my heart was free. I rose, went forth and followed thee." My deliverance in Jesus ignited a desire to live like he was at the center of my identity. Not as a way of denying my ethnic identity, but by submitting that to him as well. The Lord determined the day of my birth, my parents, and my ethnic and cultural context (Acts 17:26). Thus, my ethnic identity is a good thing. It's just not *the* thing. My divine dissatisfaction stemmed from the way that we, in the body of Christ, live as if our ethnic identity is the thing that matters most. To be absolutely clear, this is not without reason for ethnic minority churches in America. For instance, the Black church in America exists as a result of white supremacy being embraced and promoted by the majority white church. The Lord cannot and will not be defeated or thrown off course by the schemes and sins of people. Therefore, he determined in eternity past to raise up a branch of his church among African Americans where they could serve him in holiness and have their dignity as image-bearers affirmed in loving community.

At the same time, humanity's diversity is rooted in God's creative genius and humanity's destiny is to live in the reality of unity in diversity with Jesus Christ as the king to whom we will all joyfully bow. This is the beautiful community that Herman Bavinck gets at when he writes,

> The image of God is much too rich for it to be fully realized in a single human being, however richly gifted that human being may be. It can only be somewhat unfolded in its depth and riches in a humanity counting billions of members . . . [The image of God] is an undeserved gift of grace that was given to the first human being immediately at the creation but at the same time is the grounding principle and germ of an altogether rich and glorious development. Only humanity in its entirety—as one complete organism, summed up under a single head, spread out over the whole earth, as prophet proclaiming the truth of God, as priest dedicating itself to God, as ruler controlling the earth and the whole of creation—only it is the fully finished image, the most telling and striking likeness of God.

The image of God is much too rich to be fully realized in a single human being, regardless of the extent of their giftedness. In her song *Enclosed by You,* singer Liz Vice asks God, "How can I contain you, when you contain everything? The house of my soul is far too small." When I look at another human being, I am looking at royalty. But I am not looking at the full measure of what it means for humanity to be God's image. I would expand Bavinck's words to say that the image of God is much too rich for it to be realized in a single race, ethnic group, or culture. There is comfort in our cultural connection. Ethnic identity feels primordial to those embedded within a given culture. That is, it feels as though it's the essence of who we are. This makes the intersection of multiple cultures challenging. In the next chapter we will explore the Scriptures for what I believe to be the source of this challenge.

> *When I look at another human being, I am looking at royalty.*

When we look back to Genesis 1:28, we hear the Lord issue a cultural mandate to our first parents when he blessed them and said, "Be fruitful and multiply and fill the earth and subdue it, and have dominion over the fish of the sea and over the birds of the heavens and over every living thing that moves on the earth." The initial commission was to cultivate the earth. Just as in creation the Lord brought order out of chaos, humanity as his image was to cultivate his world to his glory. That is to say, we were going to be culture makers. It is inherent to who we are as his image. What's more, God intended cultural diversity over the world even if sin had never entered the picture.

All culture, as my friend Dr. Carl Ellis likes to say, begins with the question, "How do we respond to God?" This is our Father's world, after all. Culture is about how we respond to the gift of God's creation. It's about what we make of the world. Not just the "stuff" or the "things" that we make, but the meaning that we make as well. Thus, before the fall, cultivating different parts of the world would result in different manifestations of culture, but without the hostility. Obviously, the cultural mandate was not and could not be an individual endeavor. The mandate is intimately connected to the Lord's command to be fruitful and multiply and fill the earth. The cultivating aspect of the command is seen in the instruction to subdue the earth. The idea of subduing here does not include an excessive use or misuse of power for personal purposes. The Hebrew word *kabash* often carries that sense (Jeremiah 34:16; Amos 8:4; Nehemiah 5:5; Esther 7:8). But God issues this command before oppression and injustice exist from the abuse of power. Here, the subjugation is to engage the world's raw resources in a way that blesses the creation (humanity in particular) and glorifies God.

So, for example, wood is not just useful for burning in order to provide heat. We're also able to create music from it. It can be shaped and formed into a drum, guitar, piano, and an array of other instruments. As we have seen before, we're not just talking about utility. We're talking about beauty. In our cultivating and creating we're imaging God. But we're only imaging him. We're constrained in our creating to using materials that already exist. Human creativity, says Simon Oliver, is a participation in the absolute, supreme, and utterly unique creativity of God in creating the universe. He continues, "At our most creative we create things that are genuinely new, that are genuinely surprising, or that open up for us new vistas, new modes of understanding, new visions of beauty." This is true now in the fallen world. Imagine how true it would've been for us without the corrupting impact of sin!

This cultivating and creating of beauty in the world necessitates community. Bavinck is right. Humanity's destiny is in community. It is in beautiful community that we image God as we live out our love for him doing what he commissioned us to do. If you want to picture the fully finished image of God you have to picture all of humanity unified in diversity under the lordship of Jesus Christ (Ephesians 1:10; Colossians 1:20) in our role as prophets proclaiming God's truth to one another and the creation in our words and deeds; as priests continually dedicating all of ourselves to God in our words and deeds; as royalty exercising dominion over the creation in our care to the glory of God.

HUMAN DESTINY: ROYAL BEAUTY IN COMMUNITY

God is committed to this vision for humanity. We see it hinted at in passages like Isaiah 61:10–62:3:

> I will greatly rejoice in the LORD;
>> my soul shall exult in my God,
> for he has clothed me with the garments of salvation;
>> he has covered me with the robe of righteousness,
> as a bridegroom decks himself like a priest with a beautiful
>> headdress,
>> and as a bride adorns herself with her jewels.
> For as the earth brings forth its sprouts,
>> and as a garden causes what is sown in it to sprout up,
> so the Lord GOD will cause righteousness and praise
>> to sprout up before all the nations.
> For Zion's sake I will not keep silent,
>> and for Jerusalem's sake I will not be quiet,
> until her righteousness goes forth as brightness,
>> and her salvation as a burning torch.
> The nations shall see your righteousness,
>> and all the kings your glory,
> and you shall be called by a new name
>> that the mouth of the LORD will give.
> You shall be a crown of beauty in the hand of the LORD,
>> and a royal diadem in the hand of your God.

When I read this passage I think to myself, "There's something to shout about!" I love it, in part, because of how intimate it is. Take a moment to dwell on these words: "For the sake of Zion I will not be silent. And for the sake of Jerusalem I will not keep quiet." At first blush it seems as though the prophet Isaiah is speaking out, but this is the declaration of the anointed one, the same one who spoke in 61:1-3 and said,

> The Spirit of the Lord GOD is upon me,
>> because the LORD has anointed me
> to bring good news to the poor;
>> he has sent me to bind up the brokenhearted,
> to proclaim liberty to the captives,
>> and the opening of the prison to those who are bound;
> to proclaim the year of the LORD's favor,
>> and the day of vengeance of our God;
>> to comfort all who mourn;
> to grant to those who mourn in Zion—
>> to give them a beautiful headdress instead of ashes,
> the oil of gladness instead of mourning,
>> the garment of praise instead of a faint spirit;
> that they may be called oaks of righteousness,
>> the planting of the LORD, that he may be glorified.

When Jesus chose to preach Isaiah 61:1-2 for his inaugural sermon (Luke 4:16-21) he laid claim to being the anointed one of this whole section of Isaiah. Jesus is the only preacher in history who has the goods to preach a sermon about himself!

On closer look, there is a dual intimacy in 61:10 between the anointed one and the Father and the anointed one and the people of promise. What does the anointed one say? "I will greatly rejoice in the LORD; My soul shall exult in my God!" What's the reason for all this joy?

It's because his God has dressed him in salvation's garments. He's wrapped him in the cloak of righteousness.

Back in Isaiah 59:14, Isaiah declares that justice has been turned back and righteousness stands far away. In 59:15, he says that the Lord saw it and it displeased him that there was no justice. So he needed to take care of the problem himself. Then the prophet writes that the Lord's own arm brought him salvation and his righteousness upheld him. He put on righteousness as a breastplate and the helmet of salvation on his head (59:16-17). By the time we arrive at 61:10, we find out that the Lord accomplishes this by transferring that clothing to the anointed one. This is the beautiful picture of the intimacy between the Father and the Son in the work of salvation. The anointed one doesn't need salvation's garments and the cloak of righteousness for his own sake. He doesn't need saving. He wears it for the sake of those who need salvation! And putting these clothes on makes him shout for joy!

My grandmother left Wilmington, North Carolina, for Harlem in 1947 as part of the Great Migration of African Americans out of the southern states trying to make a better life for their families. One by one, each of her six children joined her in New York City, my mother arriving in 1952. So I was surrounded by a large family during my childhood years and holidays were always boisterous occasions as family and friends congregated at my house. When Easter rolled around, we knew at least two things: my grandmother would purchase us tickets to some kind of play on Broadway and the boys in the family would get new suits while the girls received new dresses. We would be decked out for Easter. I had more joy about my new suit than I did about the resurrection.

> *The anointed one doesn't need salvation's garments and the cloak of righteousness for his own sake. He doesn't need saving.*

New clothes make us feel good. They lift our spirits. And the anointed one shouts for joy over his new wardrobe. But his joy lies in the fact that his clothes are for us! He's wearing salvation's garments for you and me! This text gives us insight into Hebrews 12:1-2,

> Therefore, since we are surrounded by so great a cloud of witnesses, let us lay aside every weight and sin which clings so closely, and let us run with endurance the race that is set before us, looking to Jesus the founder and perfecter of our faith, who for the *joy* that was set before him endured the cross, despising the shame. (emphasis added)

Jesus' joy comes from the Father's act of dressing him in garments of salvation and righteousness for us. But it goes even further than that. His intimacy is not just with God, it's also with his people. So he says in 62:1, "For the sake of Zion I will not be silent. For the sake of Jerusalem I will not keep quiet. Until her righteousness goes forth like a bright light, and her salvation burns like a torch!"(author's translation).

In the 1980s, Run-DMC released a song about people who talk too much with the lyrics, "Twenty-five hours, eight days a week, thirteen months out the year is when you speak . . . You talk too much then you never shut up. I said you talk too much, homeboy, you never shut up!" Well, the anointed one is saying, "I refuse to shut up. Twenty-five hours, eight days a week, thirteen months out of the year I'm gonna keep on speaking. I will not close my mouth until Zion's righteousness is as bright as the sun!"

Who's the anointed one talking to? He's talking to his Father, saying I'm not going to rest until this picture of beauty and glory is fully painted. Are you able to hear the anointed one telling you to rejoice over the fact that he's working, that he has the Father's ear and will not close his mouth until righteousness and justice shine brightly throughout the earth?

Look at the picture of beauty that's painted for us in this passage. In chapter 61, the anointed one says he will replace the ashes and mourning of his people with a beautiful headdress and the oil of gladness. But the imagery of beauty changes in 62:3: "You shall be a crown of beauty in the hand of the LORD, and a royal diadem in the hand of your God." You're not going to wear a beautiful crown; you're going to *be* a beautiful crown. You won't wear a royal diadem; you'll *be* a royal diadem. The anointed one wears the garments of righteousness and salvation with joy because he can see the end. He can see the fulness of time and the royal beauty of his people. This is the vision of the redeemed shining together in radiant regal beauty. It is what John picks up on in Revelation 19:6-8 when God opens his ears to hear what seemed to be the voice of a great multitude, like the roar of many waters.

> Then I heard what seemed to be the voice of a great multitude, like the roar of many waters and like the sound of mighty peals of thunder, crying out, "Hallelujah! For the Lord our God the Almighty reigns. Let us rejoice and exult and give him the glory, for the marriage of the Lamb has come, and his Bride has made herself ready; it was granted her to clothe herself with fine linen, bright and pure"—for the fine linen is the righteous deeds of the saints.

And again, in Revelation 21:9-11:

> Then came one of the seven angels who had the seven bowls full of the seven last plagues and spoke to me, saying, "Come, I will show you the Bride, the wife of the Lamb." And he carried me away in the Spirit to a great, high mountain, and showed me the holy city Jerusalem coming down out of heaven from God, having the glory of God, its radiance like a most rare jewel, like a jasper, clear as crystal.

The royal beauty of the people of God pictured for us in Isaiah 62 and carried through in Revelation is a balm for our soul. This vision is actually hard to believe if our eyes are only set on the trauma-inducing reality of our divisions. When we're in the middle of the mess, when we are struggling in the church and in our communities, can we have the kind of vision that looks at image-bearers and sees the end? The kind that sees the reunion and reunification of humanity brought together in the royal beauty that the anointed one promises? Alec Motyer captures this truth when he writes, "To be in his hand is to be kept, guarded and upheld; to be a crown is to be that which expresses kingliness—not the exercise of royal power (the wearing of a crown) but the possession of royal worth and dignity. The Lord's people will be the sign that he is King." Isaiah doesn't simply say we will be a beautiful crown, a royal diadem. He says we'll be a beautiful crown in the hand of the Lord! We'll be a royal diadem in the hand of God, the sign that he is King. And this beauty will never fade, the brilliance will never dull because the Lord makes and keeps us beautiful, upholding us in beauty.

PART 2

RESTORING AND CULTIVATING OUR BEAUTIFUL COMMUNITY

5

YOUR BEAUTIFUL CROWN HAS COME DOWN FROM YOUR HEAD

Ghettoization of Humanity

Jake is a self-described conservative Republican who works in politics for a living. He's white and serves as a deacon at his church. Although his church is racially diverse, he assumed that his Black brothers and sisters were politically conservative like him because they were committed Christians. "I didn't really think about it," he said. "They love the Lord," he thought, "they must be conservative." On one occasion, he posted an image of President Barack Obama on Facebook with the Bill of Rights under the president's feet. He said, "I remember at the time thinking maybe I shouldn't post it, but that was more of a passing thought. Yeah, it's fine. Everybody would understand this." Well, everybody didn't understand. That night, in response to his post, a Black woman from the church posted on her Facebook page, "I can't believe somebody gets a pass on being a racist bigot because they're an officer in our church." She didn't name any names, but it wasn't hard to figure out who she was talking about.

He never saw the post, but three people texted him to say, "I think she's talking about you." Then he said, "I thought maybe she is." He wondered, "How come three people immediately thought of me when she posted this? That was a little disconcerting." How would you respond to a situation like this? Would you respond angrily about being called a racist bigot in public? Would you act defensively and give her a piece of your mind to tell her why she's wrong about you?

Jake's first instinct was to have a conversation with her, not on Facebook but face-to-face. He couldn't imagine a scenario where the label "racist bigot" would fit him, yet there it was.

He called her on the phone and said, "Let me ask you this. You posted something on your Facebook page last night. I never saw it, but can I ask, was that about me?" She said, "Absolutely it was. I don't know how you figured out it was you, but yes." They talked for an hour and he invited her to meet him for lunch the following week. Jake said that during that lunch, "For the first time in my life, I just let her talk and I listened. She said things about some of my posts and my views that I had no idea could be interpreted that way. It was the first time I stepped out of myself, saw myself from her perspective. I thought, man, maybe she's not alone. Maybe there's a whole church of people that think somehow I'm racist or bigoted because I'm a conservative and support Republican policies."

It was a turning point in his thinking. It was the first time he invited someone to share honestly how they felt about him. He began to talk with others in the church, asking them what they thought of his views. He started bumping into more and more people at his church who supported President Obama. His political language began to change the more he saw people in his church he loved because they loved Jesus, despite having a political perspective that differed from his own. He said, "I'm still a conservative. I still believe in conservative principles for the most part, but man, there's a humility with which I hold my political views that I never had before. Because, I'm like, if [my brother] loves Jesus, is a man of faith and he loves Obama, man, I must be missing something."

While his story is less than a few years old, this kind of conflict is ancient. We were made to image God as beautiful community, but sin ruptured our communion and polarization has been our story ever since. As we said earlier, fragmentation is not God's story, but it does tell humanity's story. Ethnic polarization, gender polarization, generational polarization, socioeconomic polarization, political polarization, national polarization—for every category of human community we are able to call out a particular polarization. It began in the Garden of Eden with the fracturing of the intimacy between Adam and Eve. Instead of owning their decision to trample on God's love, they placed blame elsewhere. This fracture expands exponentially in Genesis 11 at the Tower of Babel, the ghettoization of humanity.

> *We were made to image God as beautiful community, but sin ruptured our communion and polarization has been our story ever since.*

FROM THE GARDEN TO THE GHETTO

We've explored the way the Lord created us to image him as beautiful community as well as the way sin brought death into the world and permeates the entire cosmos. Instead of unity in diversity and diversity in unity, we find more examples of militant disunity in the human story. We find what I call "ghetto living." By ghetto, I don't mean a run-down, densely populated urban area characterized by blight, crime, and poverty. I'm talking about ghetto as an environment where a group of people live or work in isolation, whether by choice or circumstance, and draw their sense of worth and dignity from their identification with that community. Biblically speaking, this kind of ghetto living has its roots in the following passage of Scripture:

Now the whole earth had one language and the same words. And as people migrated from the east, they found a plain in the land of Shinar and settled there. And they said to one another, "Come, let us make bricks, and burn them thoroughly." And they had brick for stone, and bitumen for mortar. Then they said, "Come, let us build ourselves a city and a tower with its top in the heavens, and let us make a name for ourselves, lest we be dispersed over the face of the whole earth." And the LORD came down to see the city and the tower, which the children of man had built. And the LORD said, "Behold, they are one people, and they have all one language, and this is only the beginning of what they will do. And nothing that they propose to do will now be impossible for them. Come, let us go down and there confuse their language, so that they may not understand one another's speech." So the LORD dispersed them from there over the face of all the earth, and they left off building the city. Therefore its name was called Babel, because there the LORD confused the language of all the earth. And from there the LORD dispersed them over the face of all the earth. (Genesis 11:1-9)

You don't have to look very hard to find bumper stickers, billboards, speeches, or posts on social media calling for peaceful coexistence, for civility. Rodney King's question from over twenty-five years ago remains iconic in this land of hostility: "Can't we all just get along?" People are left frustrated that we're unable to come together as a human race and create a peaceful and civil coexistence.

We don't actually have to imagine what life would be like if we all just got along. Genesis 11:1-9 portrays for us a time in human history when everyone had the same language and spoke the same words. There was genuine unity and solidarity. In Genesis 11:1 Moses tells us that everyone had one language and spoke the same words. No confusion. No hostility. Humanity migrated together from the east and settled down in the land of Shinar (Mesopotamia). Here's the problem with this unity. They begin their cooperative urban development project in verse 3, but verse 2 reveals that their solidarity is one of rebellion against God's direct command! After the Flood narrative in Genesis 6–9, God repeats the command he gave humanity in Genesis 1:28, "be fruitful and multiply and fill the earth" (Genesis 9:1). Let's not miss the fact that in both instances, the command is preceded with God's blessing humanity for fulfilment of his command. Yet, what do we find humanity doing? They consciously and bluntly declare their rejection of God by rejecting his command. "We refuse to fill the earth. Instead, we're going to settle down right here."

They were not ignorant of God's command. They couldn't claim the excuse that they didn't know what they were supposed to do. Notice as well that we don't find the serpent here like we did in Genesis 3, tempting humanity to disobey God's Word. Humanity as one big happy family happily worked together against its creator. The term translated "from the east" or "eastward" in verse 2 marks a separation in Genesis. It conveys the reality that the people of Babel are outside of God's blessing.

We see this reality expressed throughout Genesis. In 3:24 when God drove Adam and Eve out of the Garden of Eden, he placed a cherubim and flaming sword at the *east* of the garden. In chapter four when Cain killed his brother, Abel, he went away from the presence of the Lord and settled in Nod, *east* of Eden. In chapter thirteen, Lot journeyed *eastward* to settle in Sodom when he separated from Abraham. By moving eastward and settling in Shinar, the big happy human family of Babel is outside of God's blessing.

That's why bumper sticker theology is fruitless. Bumper sticker theology that simply calls for coexistence cannot actually do anything. Even if by some means we were able to achieve corporate civility and peaceful coexistence through our own efforts, we would remain a corrupt people unified only by our sinful rebellion against God. Like the actions described in 11:3-4 tell us, we would express our solidarity by trying to use God's gracious gifts to usurp his authority and make a name for ourselves.

As chapter 11 opens, humanity has one language, speaking a unified message, and they express their solidarity in a construction project (11:3-4). There's no attempt to even fake obedience to God. This is the warp, the dysfunction, the disordering that sin creates within. The sinful human heart drives us to find significance through our own achievements. It fuels our desire to make a name for ourselves apart from God. It feeds our craving for glory and fame. In their futile efforts to establish significance by their own achievements, the people of Babel rally to make bricks and mortar in order to build a city with a tower that rises into the heavens.

In the ancient Near East, cities were not designed primarily for living. They were intended for religious and public purposes. In Mesopotamian culture, where Babel would have been located, they employed their technology to build a city with a central focus on a ziggurat. It was meant to be an inseparable part of the city. Sometimes the temple complex was the entire city. Bruce Waltke describes it this way:

> Like Jacob's staircase (see Gen. 28:12), the ziggurat mountain, with its roots in the earth and its lofty top in the clouds, served in mythopoeic thought as a gate to heaven. This humanly created mountain gave humanity access to heaven (28:17) and served as a convenient stairway for the gods to come down into their temple and into the city.

In other words, the people of Babel are contesting with God himself.

The city reveals the fact that the sinful human heart desires, above all, to wrest the throne from God himself. This is insanity. We are royalty, but we are vice-regents. That's not enough for us! Thus, we still pervert God's good gift. We still desire to make a name for ourselves. We still want to find significance by our own achievements. Apart from the Spirit of Christ working in us, we cannot think of any other glory than our own. Notice in 11:5-7 that the human commitment to build in solidarity contrasts with God's commitment to deconstruct by way of confusing speech.

Why are we told that the Lord came down to see the city and the tower (11:5)? Was he somehow surprised by what was going on? Was he lacking in some knowledge about the building project and needed to get a closer look so that he could decide what to do about it? No, absolutely not. The reason we're told that the Lord came down to see the city and the tower is that it emphasizes the futility of human efforts against God. By human standards, the city and tower were impressive, a work like no other. It was the result of all of humanity putting their minds together for a singular purpose. They thought that such a technological breakthrough would enable them to travel into the heavenly realm where God dwelled. Together, as one, they believed their strength and intelligence unmatched. Yet, for all of their effort, for all of their building success, their tower remained so puny and impotent that God has to come down to see it. Their best efforts at reaching the heavens don't even come close.

We're still striving to obtain significance through technological advancements. We continue to insist that if we can just find a cure for the latest disease, we'll be closer to heaven. If we can utilize technology to improve the quality of life, to extend life capacity, to create more materially prosperous lives, then we will prove that we do not need God. Then we will receive all of the glory, fame, and significance. This is not an anti-advancement rant. Lord knows, I'm grateful for medical advancements and improvements in technology that lead to better human health and flourishing. What I am speaking to is the futility of trying to make our own way apart from God, the futility of thinking so arrogantly that we could possibly do anything worthy of God's recognition apart from him working in and through us—apart from us working for his glory and not our own.

God comes down in judgment (vv. 6-7) and effectively creates ghettos by confusing our language so that we can't understand one another. And even in God's judgment here there is mercy. When the Lord says in v.6, "They are one people, and they have all one language, and this is only the beginning of what they will do. And nothing that they propose to do will now be impossible for them," he mercifully moves to restrain our sin by confusing our language. There is grace in the judgment of Babel. How much worse would this world be if God allowed us to continue to be united in our sinful purposes? The willful rebellion of humanity against God's explicit command resulted in the use of all our faculties united for an impossible goal. We were joined together to establish ourselves as God, with all authority and power.

What it means is that in spite of what it looks like, this world ain't as bad as it could be! If we all "just got along," we'd be just getting along in trying to overthrow God together. Therefore, by divine judgment he creates ghettos.

God had blessed humanity (Genesis 1:28; 9:1), and his plan was for humanity to be a blessing in the earth. The refusal to be fruitful and multiply and fill the earth seemed to threaten that plan. But God will not be thwarted! If his mandate to fill the earth was going to be accomplished God was going to have to do it himself, in spite of us, not because of us. In judgment and mercy, he confused our language. They were trying to make a name for themselves, and the name they end up earning is the name God gives them in verse 8, "confusion." Now, because they can't understand each other they have to stop building the tower. They have to spread out over the earth. More accurately, v. 9 tells us that the Lord dispersed them from there over the earth. As a result of the confusion we no longer trust each other. And the spirit of

Babel is still with us. We are still in solidarity against God, yet this solidarity is expressed in isolated communities. These ghettos, because they are in rebellion against God, are also naturally against each other. So, what happens far too often is that we understand our human dignity and value as coming from isolated community. And we love our ghettos, our ethnic ghettos, our social ghettos, our cultural ghettos, our economic ghettos, our academic ghettos. And we love them to a fault. When we see cultural and ethnic differences, we don't embrace our dissimilarity, we immediately distrust. We instinctively reject and often mock because we're still confused and don't understand each other.

Can I tell you something? You have no idea how much your understanding of what it means to be human, to live a good life, to experience love, to be a friend, husband, wife, and worker is shaped by your ghetto. We're blind to its many facets because we have swum in its water our whole lives. And when we see or experience something different, our first impulse is to react in judgment of that difference.

RACISM AND THE AMERICAN GHETTO

Our ghettoization has deadly consequences. Racism is one of those consequences. Indeed, the creation of different races is full-blown ghettoization and idolatry. Why did racist ideas come to be? Ibram X. Kendi defines a racist idea as any concept that regards one racial group as inferior or superior to another racial group in any way. He writes that he used to believe a popular folktale of racism "that ignorant and hateful people had produced racist ideas, and that these racist people had instituted racist policies." But then, after he examined America's most influential racist ideas, he found the historical evidence yields a different story. Rather than racial ignorance and hate leading to the creation of racist ideas and racial discrimination, the inverse is true. Racial discrimination drove the creation of racist ideas which led to racial ignorance and hate. He points out that "racially discriminatory policies have usually sprung from economic, political, and cultural self-interests, self-interests that are constantly changing." The point of contact between the ghettoization of humanity and Kendi's discovery is that racially discriminatory policies came to be in order to serve cultural and other self-interests.

Put in theological terms, our racialized society is an outworking of our ghettoization at Babel. And the devastating reality is that groups of people still seek to serve the interests of their ghetto. The idea of different races is a social construct. It was created by humanity, but it is not a reflection of the beautiful image-bearing creative genius we discussed in the last chapter. It is strictly relegated to the sinful and depraved purposes of exploitation and oppression. To be clear, it served as a justification to overtake and enslave whole people groups. Race, claims Dr. Korie Edwards, is central to the structure of American life and the everyday lives of Americans. Indeed, whiteness is the cornerstone of the racial system in the United States. She describes race as the basis of social systems that distribute rewards. People placed in the dominant stratum establish the racial classifications and have greater access to and possession of society's valuable resources along with more power to reserve them for their group.

Bearing this in mind leads some Christians to argue that we shouldn't even talk about race or use the word since it's a manmade concept. Using the term only serves to further divide us. There's only one race—the human race—so shouldn't we just categorize differences between people with terminology like "ethnicity"? In a word, no. I believe that Scripture compels us to speak the truth about the primary way our ghettoization has manifested itself in the American context. Discarding the word "race" would make it easier to ignore the devastating and deadly impact of racialized ghettoization. Further, we would fool ourselves into thinking that this is just a problem of the past. As my brother Dr. Jarvis Williams puts it, race is a biological fiction, but a sociological fact. Kendi's point about the changing nature of racialization in America reinforces what Christian Smith and Michael Emerson explained in 2000 when they wrote,

> The framework we here use—racialization—reflects that [post-Civil Rights era] adaptation. It understands that racial practices that reproduce racial division in the contemporary United States (1) are increasingly covert, (2) are embedded in normal operations of institutions, (3) avoid direct racial terminology, and (4) are invisible to most Whites.

In a racialized society, racist ideas become embedded in individuals, institutions, and systems. They manifest themselves in both aggressively active ways and subtly passive ways. However, every manifestation has the capacity for deadly violence. Discriminatory housing and loan practices can destroy lives for generations.

We have lived in ghettos ever since Babel, finding our sense of value and worth in our group. But whatever your group may be, it's only a facet of the human experience. What's most tragic is that Jesus' church has a ghetto-busting responsibility, but it has, like the people of Babel, ignored that command.

In a racialized society, racist ideas become embedded in individuals, institutions, and systems.

I am a minister in the Presbyterian Church in America (PCA). Currently, our denomination has almost 4,900 ministers. Around 50 are Black, 40 Hispanic, and 480 Asian. Two are First Nations. No non-white minority group by itself comprises 10 percent of the ministers. But don't mistake this situation for a fluke of history. The ministerial makeup of my denomination didn't form in a vacuum. The history of race and racism in the PCA is ugly. In fact, we're regularly forced to explore the way our theological and ecclesial practices lead to the exclusion of people of color. We have to press into the way our tradition leads to boundary policing that serves as a race test preventing people of color from experiencing a true home in our context.

In 2007 Doris Salcedo contributed a work of art to the Tate Modern Museum in Britain, which took the form of a crack in the floor of the museum. She titled the work *Shibboleth* and it is described as

a reference to Judges 12 where the Gileadites sifted out their enemies by asking them to say the word, "shibboleth," which sounded different in different dialects. Saying "sibboleth" became a death sentence. The term has since come to mean a custom, phrase, or use of language that acts as a test of belonging to a particular social group. It is an exclusionary tool. Salcedo cracked open the floor in an effort to make visible the hidden ways in which we police our boundaries—the impossible tests that we give to others in order to maintain our own comfort or sense of security.

I've been a part of the PCA almost twenty years so my critique comes from the inside. And it's only one example of the many ecclesial ghettos that mimic the world as though we do not have a Christ who calls us to pursue reconciliation. In her 2018 Covenant College commencement address Dr. Elissa Yukiko Weichbrodt referenced Salcedo's piece in the following way:

Sometimes we believe that dignity is a pie to be divvied up among us. We worry that if we grant dignity to one group's suffering or accounting of history then there is less available for us. But this is foolish. We make God small when the reverse should be the case. For, after all, if Jesus is coming back to make all the sad things untrue, then the more sad things we know, the *bigger* Jesus must be to undo them. The cracks are already there. Calling out the brokenness does not diminish Jesus's power. It *magnifies* it.

How do we get out of the ghetto? What's the solution to so much brokenness? That's what chapters eight, nine, and ten of this book are about. But here's the quick answer: it's nothing short of the blood of Jesus. It's in the community of the redeemed that we should see the dividing line of hostility broken down (Ephesians 2:14).

What does this mean on the ground in our day-to-day lives? It means you have to walk with humility. You have to know that when we're talking about and engaging the issues that still divide us in this land (and in the church), your thoughts are informed by the ghetto that formed you in ways that you're simply unaware of. And we need to be shaped and reshaped by other brothers and sisters in the Lord who come out of different ghettos if we're going to learn to love well and strive for justice and righteousness in our communities. I used to say to the church I served that God was giving us a particular kind of grace as we pursued crosscultural living. I knew that we would regularly offend one another because we speak different languages. That is, we come from different ghettos. When we offend one another, that grace takes the form of asking ourselves, "Why am I offended? Is the heart of this issue really about my preferences and desires that have been shaped by my ghetto? Would the Lord have me die to this for the sake of the unity of the Spirit in the bond of peace?"

What I'm about to say may not be popular, but in America the greater burden of dying to preferences is borne by those in the majority white culture. Among the many points we can make about America's founding, we must include the establishment of a white cultural normativity. Its existence has made the norm for minorities in America to embrace discomfort in majority culture contexts—an experience no less true in the church. As I mentioned earlier, we have no idea the depths to which our expectations, desires, preferences, and predilections are informed by our ghetto. When your ghetto is the norm, your default position is to expect others to conform to your way of being.

Research of multiracial churches bears this out. I am fully aware that engaging the topic of whiteness triggers a defensiveness among white people as well as a discomfort among some non-white people. But this is the elephant in the room for the American church.

So, what is whiteness? Dr. Edwards helpfully points out three inter-dependent dimensions of whiteness:

1. *White structural advantage*—Whites disproportionately control or influence political parties, the legal system, government agencies, industry, and business.

2. White structural advantage facilitates *white normativity*. What this means is that divergence from the norm signifies deviant practices or understandings.

3. *White transparency*—Whites tend not to think about norms; behaviors, experiences, or perspectives that are white-specific. There is a lack of awareness that their race has consequences for their lives. Consequently, it is difficult for whites to explain what it means to be white.

> *When your ghetto is the norm, your default position is to expect others to conform to your way of being.*

This is the elephant in the room because the default perspective, even among people of color, is that of white norms in racially and ethnically diverse church contexts. Dr. Edwards likens it to adding rainbow sprinkles to a dish of vanilla ice cream. The vanilla ice cream is still the strongest flavor you experience. I've experienced this in diverse churches where I've worshipped and in the church I pastored. This is why I say that there is a particular need for white Christians to develop a deeper cultural self-awareness and a willingness to die to maintaining some of those cultural norms for the sake of pursuing unity in diversity.

We must realize that getting out of our ghettos isn't free. It'll cost you. You'll have to examine your preferences. You'll have to regularly embrace being more curious than confident when you're in a situation involving diversity and difference. If you're a part of the majority culture, you'll have to learn how to listen to and learn under the influence of non-majority culture people. If you're a part of a minority culture, you'll need to learn how to trust majority culture folks—especially if your corporate/collective history is covered in wounds.

Make no mistake, getting out of the ghetto is uncomfortable, but it's close to God's heart. Revelation 5 describes Jesus Christ as worthy to receive power, wealth, wisdom, might, honor, glory, and blessing because he, by his blood, ransomed people from every tribe, tongue, people, and nation. God's plan will not be thwarted. That vision will come to pass, not through the United Nations, but through the church of the living God empowered by the Spirit of God.

6

I WILL BEAUTIFY MY BEAUTIFUL HOUSE

Identity and Formation

I n their book *Against All Odds: The Struggle for Integration in Religious Organizations,* Brad Christerson, Korie Edwards, and Michael Emerson recount their engagement with several current and former members of a predominately Filipino church. This church became ethnically diverse because the founding pastor had an ethnically diverse network of friends. They found that in spite of the efforts of the church "to be warm and embracing, the biggest obstacle in its five-year history seems to have been that many of its members feel socially isolated." This feeling resulted in several members leaving the congregation. The vast majority of the non-Filipino members cited a lack of connection as their reason for leaving. The importance of people experiencing belonging and the struggle for it to substantively take place in interracial religious organizations led them to conclude that interracial religious organizations are inherently unstable.

On March 10, 2018, the *New York Times* published an article titled, "A Quiet Exodus: Why Black Worshipers Are Leaving White Evangelical Churches." The author, Campbell Robertson writes,

In the last couple of decades, there had been signs, however modest, that eleven o'clock on Sunday morning might cease to be the most segregated hour in America. "Racial reconciliation" was the talk of conferences and the subject of formal resolutions. Large Christian ministries were dedicated to the aim of integration, and many black Christians decided to join white-majority congregations. Some went as missionaries, called by God to integrate. Others were simply drawn to a different worship style—short, conveniently timed services that emphasized a personal connection to God.

He argues that the 2016 election of President Donald Trump was a turning point, when statistics showed that white evangelicals voted for him in larger numbers than they had voted for any previous presidential candidate. It was a turning point, yes, but not an originating point. Black evangelicals were pained by the ongoing racial injustice as they watched the killing of unarmed black men and women by law enforcement, circumstances met with silence from their white pastors. By contrast, terrorist-related tragedies in places like Paris and Brussels incited prayers for those afflicted and mourning. The tension was building long before the election.

When Christians of color heard white evangelicals cheering the outcome of the election "reassuring uneasy fellow worshipers with talk of abortion and religious liberty, about how politics is the art of compromise rather than the ideal," it left many bewildered. It left them wondering how voters could so easily overlook the president's comments about Mexican immigrants, NFL players protesting police brutality, and his birther crusade against President Obama. Michael Emerson, quoted in the article, claims that the 2016 presidential election was the single most harmful event to the whole movement of reconciliation in at least the past thirty years.

On March 11, 2019, Dr. Anthony Bradley published an article in *Fathom* magazine titled, "The Great Commission Christianity Keeps Blacks Away From Evangelicalism." In the article, Dr. Bradley explains how since 1994 he's been researching evangelicalism's inability to successfully integrate its churches and institutions following the Civil Rights Movement. He makes a distinction in the article between Great Commission Christianity and Cosmic Redemptive Christianity. In Great Commission Christianity, the gospel is "the announcement of the good news of Jesus' work to restore image-bearers to the rightful worship of God." This, he claims, is not a wrong view, but a limited one. "Its hyper-focus on saving individuals and the work of the church says nothing about the redemption of creation, which God is also reconciling to himself through Christ." Cosmic Redemptive Christianity, on the other hand, understands the gospel this way: "Through the person and work of Jesus Christ, God fully accomplishes salvation for us, rescuing us from judgment for sin into fellowship with him, and then restores the creation in which we can enjoy our new life together with him forever." What appears to be a subtle difference has significant implications. He points out that Great Commission Christianity has no need to engage social justice issues since it doesn't preach a redemption that considers all of creation primary. I would add that Great Commission Christianity only selectively engages social issues (i.e., abortion). However, Cosmic Redemptive Christianity is embodied in the Black church and the Reformed tradition. Both understand that "the gospel, at its core, is about God calling his people to himself *and* the liberation of creation." Dr. Bradley references the quiet exodus from the *New York Times* article, claiming that the exodus will continue as long as the truncated Great Commission Christianity remains the prevailing center of evangelicalism.

In order to be in community, we have to experience belonging, a sense of being at home.

When you consider the polarization embodied by the three twenty-first century examples cited above, the hope of reconciliation seems dire. The problem of the divided church in

America and the forces that keep us apart isn't relegated to a bygone, racialized society. It's all still current, right here right now. Again, fragmentation has characterized humanity's story since Genesis 3 and our attempts to break out of the ghetto living inaugurated in Genesis 11 seem to be futile. The ghettos we belong to shape and form our identity for better and worse. In order to be in community, we have to experience belonging, a sense of being at home. The data led the authors of *Against All Odds* to conclude that there is an inherent instability to our ghetto-breaking efforts in the church. The fractures that divide us across race, class, and culture often run deep and can make reconciliation in the here and now a tenuous venture. What are we to do?

THE PROMISE OF GOD

In his poem "Pied Beauty," Jesuit priest Gerard Manley Hopkins opens with the words, "Glory be to God for dappled things." To be dappled is to be variegated, exhibiting different colors. The dappled things for which the author glorifies God are the skies, fish, finches, the landscape, and the like. All of the created variety in this world points to the glory and grandeur of God. The Lord loves difference. As much as it feels like our ecclesial press toward beautiful community has us spinning our wheels, our hope isn't based on our progress. It's based on God's promise. We press based on promise.

> *All of the created variety in this world points to the glory and grandeur of God.*

Every major epoch of judgment or curse in the book of Genesis has a corresponding covenantal promise to undo the effects of that curse. Human sin and rebellion bring judgment from God's hand. If left to ourselves, that judgment would be the final word. The only way for there to be a different final word is for God to declare it. We find the Lord promising to bless humanity and his world with a blessing that's related to the judgment.

In Genesis 3 as the Lord declares his judgment for the sin of our first parents, he speaks a word of promise—the first gospel—in 3:15. The serpent's offspring will bruise the heel of the woman's offspring, but her offspring will deal a death blow to the head of the serpent's offspring. In Genesis 6–8, God's judgment falls on humanity in the re-creation event of the flood. The word of promise comes in 8:21-22:

> I will never again curse the ground because of man, for the intention of man's heart is evil from his youth. Neither will I ever again strike down every living creature as I have done. While the earth remains, seedtime and harvest, cold and heat, summer and winter, day and night, shall not cease.

The same pattern holds in Genesis 11 after the ghettoization of humanity at Babel. What is the Lord's response to the judgment rendered at Babel? At the end of the chapter (11:28), we're introduced to a man named Abram who moves to center stage at the beginning of chapter 12.

> Now the LORD said to Abram, "Go from your country and your kindred and your father's house to the land that I will show you. And I will make of you a great nation, and I will bless you and make your name great, so that you will be a blessing. I will bless those who bless you, and him who dishonors you I will curse, and in you all the families of the earth shall be blessed." (Genesis 12:1-3)

Do you hear what the Lord is promising here? He says he will bless all the families of the earth through Abraham. What is that blessing? The promised blessing is not just the Great Commission Christianity that Dr. Bradley wrote about. The blessing is that the Lord will bring back together all of the families he separated by his judgment at Babel through Abraham's seed. God is committed to the realization of beautiful community for humanity, a promise fulfilled in Jesus Christ. He is the great reconciler and he gives us the ministry of reconciliation in his name.

In Jesus' high priestly prayer in John 17, he makes a request of the Father. In verses 6-19 he prays for his disciples, particularly those who followed him in his earthly ministry. But in verse 20 he begins to pray for a different group.

> I do not ask for these only, but also for those who will believe in me through their word, that they may all be one, just as you, Father, are in me, and I in you, that they also may be in us, so that the world may believe that you have sent me. The glory that you have given me I have given to them, that they may be one even as we are one, I in them and you in me, that they may become perfectly one, so that the world may know that you sent me and loved them even as you loved me. (John 17:20-23)

He is looking toward the future and praying for us, the ones who believe in him! What is chief on his mind? Our unity and our love for one another. Three times in these three verses he prays that we would be one, that there would be a reversal of the fragmentation that defines human life and relationships. The purpose of Christ bringing us into the glory of God is our unity (17:22). Please do not miss this. The necessity of our being united in beautiful community stretches back beyond the promise of Genesis 12 to the declaration of the *imago Dei* in Genesis 1:26. This is apparent in Jesus' prayer here.

He says, "May they be one, just as you, Father, *are in me, and I in you.*" Then he says, "The glory that you have given me I have given them, that they may be one *even as we are one.*" He's not picking his desire for our unity out of thin air. Do you hear what is on our Savior's mind as he prays? It's the *Shema!* "Hear, O Israel, the Lord our God is *one.*" The necessity of our unity is rooted in the unity of our God. Jesus desires to see his church reflecting the unity of our God. The Spirit of God is given to us for this purpose (Ephesians 1:13-14). What's more, Jesus says that our unity is the evidence to the world that he is real!

In other words, the church's most powerful witness to the world that Jesus is real isn't signs and wonders like miraculous healings. No, it's the supernatural life of God's people united in beautiful diverse community! Our theology of reconciliation is trinitarian. To refuse to pursue unity in diversity as a redeemed people is to fundamentally neglect what it means for us to be the image of God. The world should look at the church in amazement and wonder, "How did that happen? How did people with such differences come together and commit to staying together in spite of the difficulty?" David Livermore believes, "Few things are as sacred and worthy of our connection with other human beings than our shared identity as image bearers of the Holy Other." By implication, according to Charles Woodley, our local churches must look better in the eyes of the world and reflect the multicultural heart of the Father. We're called out of the ghetto, out of fragmentation and polarization, to a new normal in Jesus Christ.

THE NEW NORMAL

Let's look at how this came to pass in the New Testament church. Centuries prior to Jesus' coming the prophet Isaiah wrote,

> In that day there will be a highway from Egypt to Assyria, and Assyria will come into Egypt, and Egypt into Assyria, and the Egyptians will worship with the Assyrians. In that day Israel will be the third with Egypt and Assyria, a blessing in the midst of the earth, whom the LORD of hosts has blessed, saying, "Blessed be Egypt my people, and Assyria the work of my hands, and Israel my inheritance." (Isaiah 19:23-25)

I imagine that these words from the prophet's mouth utterly dumbfounded the people of Israel. The Lord is promising that their two worst enemies would become their brothers and sisters! Apparently, a day was coming when the people of Israel, the Egyptians, and the Assyrians would hold hands and sing, "We are family!" to the glory of God! In this passage, Egypt and Assyria actually represent the whole world, not just those two nations. Acts 2 is one of the places in the New Testament where we find Genesis 12 and Isaiah 19:23-25 come to pass in the church.

What may be described as the first multinational worship service in the New Testament took place on the Day of Pentecost. However, the worship of God brought confusion before it brought clarity. It was a scene like none other. All of the disciples, presumably the 120 mentioned in Acts 1:15, are together in the house. The Day of Pentecost has come. This is the day that Jesus told them to wait for, the day that they would be clothed with power from on high (Luke 24:49; Acts 1:8). As they are gathered, still devoted to prayer (Acts 1:14), the Holy Spirit arrives in dramatic fashion. A sound like the mighty driving of the wind fills the entire house. Individual tongues like fire appear resting on each of them. Luke says that they were all filled with the Holy Spirit, which resulted in their speaking other languages.

The coming of the Holy Spirit was not a private matter. It was a public declaration to the nations that the kingdom of God has come. How large was the crowd in Jerusalem? Luke doesn't say, but the delegation of international representatives is unmatched: "Parthians and Medes and Elamites and residents of Mesopotamia, Judea and Cappadocia, Pontus and Asia, Phrygia and Pamphylia, Egypt and the parts of Libya belonging to Cyrene, and visitors from Rome, both Jews and proselytes, Cretans and Arabians" (Acts 2:9-11). What did they hear? The sound of the disciples declaring the mighty works of God. What they experienced left them confused, astonished, amazed, and perplexed. It left them either utterly confused or certain the disciples were drunk (Acts 2:12-13). To bring clarity, conviction, and resolve, Peter rises to preach (2:14-36).

The message that these people from every nation needed to understand was that the end had come, the end that marked a new beginning. That new beginning was the lavish pouring out of the Spirit of God. Peter tells them that what they see might be new, but it's not unexpected. He explains to his multinational audience that all of what they witnessed was rooted in God's promise through the prophet Joel (2:17-21). The coming of the Holy Spirit was a public declaration that the kingdom of God had come. God would fill his people with his Spirit for the purpose of kingdom mission—to reverse the tragic effects of Babel. The expression of unity in humanity would be for the praise and glory of God, not for the establishment of people's own kingdom in rebellion against his rule.

Luke's description of this multinational audience is not a passing remark. It is actually key! Yes, this multinational audience came to Jerusalem because they were religiously bound by a commitment to Judaism. But few stayed that way. Three thousand souls were added to the church that day (2:41). The multinational audience is transformed into the multinational body of Christ. Their commitment as such went beyond the day of Pentecost. They became devoted not only to the apostles' teaching and corporate worship (2:42), but to one another as well (2:44-45).

In *From Every People and Nation,* Daniel Hays makes the important point that biblical scholarship has tended to overlook much of the ethnic diversity in the New Testament world. And we have the same tendency. In our connected world we clearly hear, see, and experience the diversity of our multinational world. We may live in an age of radical multinational connection due to development of new social media and technology, but there remains a drought of multinational communion. How often do we look at, study, and preach on a biblical passage like Acts 2 and miss the multinational communion? How often do we read Peter's sermon and the people's response and fail to find our hearts pierced by the dearth of multinational communion in the contemporary American church?

The multinational communion we see in Acts 2:42-47 set the trajectory for the church's new normal. Perhaps we miss its significance because the New Testament regularly categorizes humanity in terms of Jew and Gentile. Hays asserts that biblical scholarship subconsciously assumes that the New Testament world consisted of only two ethnic groups: Jews and Greco-Roman Gentiles. But people in the Greco-Roman world of the New Testament were neither mono-national nor mono-ethnic. While there was definitely a Greco-Roman culture, there was not really any Greco-Roman ethnic group. So while it may be simple, and even sometimes useful, to categorize people as either Jew or Gentile, it does not go far enough when examining God's work in the New Testament. In other words, God is not simply interested in reconciling two categories of humanity. His desire is for all nations.

Even more, the growing multiethnicity in American communities is only a return to the reality of the Greco-Roman world of the New Testament. Hays describes the types of events that took place, influencing the ethnic makeup of the region.

> Migrations and invasions occurred, such as that by the Celts into Macedonia and Asia Minor. Merchant-driven colonization occurred. Jews were scattered throughout the region: Roman soldiers and foreign auxiliary soldiers retired and settled in areas away from their homes; and slaves were captured from a variety of areas of the Roman frontier and transferred throughout the Empire to be incorporated into the diverse mix of peoples that inhabited the cities of the first century AD.

Jerusalem's large and diverse mix of peoples heard the disciples proclaiming the mighty works of God. They heard Peter preach the message of the gospel of Jesus Christ for the nations—for them. Peter makes sure to point out that "it shall come to pass that everyone who calls upon the name of the Lord shall be saved" (Acts 2:21). Then, after the people heard what Peter had to say, they were cut to the heart. They asked Peter and the apostles, "What shall we do?" Peter says, "Repent and be baptized every one of you in the name of Jesus Christ for the forgiveness of your sins, and you will receive the gift of the Holy Spirit. For the promise is for you and for your children and for all who are far off, everyone whom the Lord our God calls to himself" (Acts 2:38-39, emphasis added).

As "every nation under heaven" came to Jerusalem, the Lord God began calling people to himself. None of the nations would be excluded. There would be one Lord, one faith, one baptism, one God and Father of all. Peter's audience that day needed to be exposed to what would become the new normal. Luke's audience needed to hear that their new normal was the fulfillment of God's promise. And we need to ask ourselves whether or not we've forsaken the new normal for something else.

The reason that the message was important for them and the question is important for us is because, while the new normal is wrought by the Spirit of God, it is extremely difficult to break out of our cultural comforts and pursue it wholeheartedly. Acts removes the veil to reveal this struggle in the church. The multinational audience in Acts 2 came together as people religiously committed to Judaism. They were either ethnically Jewish or converts to Judaism. In spite of their commonality, discrimination quickly reared its head in the early church.

In Acts 6, as the disciples were multiplying, a complaint arose from the Hellenists against the Hebrews (Acts 6:1). The complaint was that the Hellenist's widows were being neglected in the daily distribution of resources for those in need. In this case, the dispute had to do with language. Some of the new disciples are native to Jerusalem and speak Aramaic as their primary language. These are the Hebrews, and they're probably the majority. The others are from the Diaspora. They aren't native to Jerusalem but came from other parts of the Roman empire. These people are the Hellenists and they spoke Greek. The struggle for the new normal of unity in diversity was very real.

This struggle continues in earnest in Acts 10:1-23 as the Holy Spirit makes it clear that the promise of Jesus' kingdom is not limited to any ethnic, socioeconomic, political, or other type of group. Peter, who preached the powerful Pentecost sermon, is confronted with his own ethnic bias when the Lord calls him to preach the gospel to a Roman centurion named Cornelius. Cornelius stands in need of gospel's comfort, and Peter stands in need of some radical theological correction. Peter has to hear Jesus' non-discrimination clause, "What God has made clean, you do not call common" (Acts 10:15). The new normal in Jesus Christ did not mean having to conform to ethnic Jewish life.

As the new normal unfolds, it begins to reach its pinnacle in Acts 11 at Antioch. Jesus chose Jerusalem to be the birthplace of Christianity, but he chose Antioch to be the nurturing place where the gospel began to go deep down into impenetrable places.

The Spirit is at work breaking down the inherent discrimination between Jew and Gentile as he builds the church. Faith in Jesus Christ has replaced overt exclusion with radical inclusion. And this radical inclusion was not going to be accomplished without conflict over previously held assumptions about people from other "tribes" being turned on their heads. In Acts 11:19, Luke takes his audience back to chapter 8 when persecution of the believers broke out. He says in verses 19-20,

> Now those who were scattered because of the persecution that arose over Stephen traveled as far as Phoenicia and Cyprus and Antioch, speaking the word to no one except Jews. But there were some of them, men of Cyprus and Cyrene, who on coming to Antioch spoke to the Hellenists also, preaching the Lord Jesus.

Native men of Cyprus and Cyrene came to Antioch and decided to break out of their cultural container and tell the good news about the Lord Jesus to non-Jews. The word *Hellenist* simply refers to a Greek speaker. Luke used it previously in chapter 6 to refer to Greek-speaking Jewish believers in the church, and in chapter 9 to refer to Greek-speaking Jews. Here, it refers to Gentiles. God is bringing some new people, unexpected people, diverse people into the church.

This beautiful painting of international evangelism and discipleship leads to the new people receiving a new name. In Antioch, Luke says, the disciples were first called "Christians." A new identity for these new people. It's no accident that we only find the word "Christian" ascribed to the followers of Jesus after the church has a massive influx of Gentiles and becomes a mixed group. Jesus has brought and is creating something new.

They became identified as people who follow Jesus Christ. So when the nations began to turn to the Lord, not only did they receive a new identity, but the church received a new identity. The importance of this new identity, this new normal, cannot be overstated. Antioch becomes the mission center for the Christian faith overtaking the mother church of Jerusalem.

The new normal reaches its pinnacle in Antioch and becomes the expectation for Christian community as churches are planted and grow in the diverse Roman cities. Ephesians 1 begins with an extended sentence in the Greek text, the apostle Paul praising God by saying, "Blessed be the God and Father of our Lord Jesus Christ, who has blessed us in Christ with every spiritual blessing in the heavenly places, even as he chose us in him before the foundation of the world, that we should be holy and blameless before him" (Ephesians 1:3-4). Paul brings the sentence to a culmination in verses 9-10 where he says that the Father has made known to us the mystery of his will, according to his purpose, in Jesus Christ, as God's plan for the fulness of time, *to unite all things in Jesus Christ, things in heaven and things on earth.* The incarnation, crucifixion, death, resurrection, ascension, and glorification of Jesus Christ reveal to us God's reunification plan to sum up everything in him. This is where Bavinck gets the imagery expressed in declaration that,

> Only humanity in its entirety—as one complete organism, summed up under a single head, spread out over the whole earth, as prophet proclaiming the truth of God, as priest dedicating itself to God, as ruler controlling the earth and the whole of creation—only it is the fully finished image, the most telling and striking likeness of God.

Here in Ephesians, what Paul emphasizes throughout the letter is that the primary evidence of God summing up everything under the lordship of Jesus is the reconciliation of Jews and Gentiles in fellowship and communion (Ephesians 2:11-22). This is the point of his prayer for the eyes of their hearts to be enlightened. He wants them to know the resurrection power of God that courses through the church for reconciliation (Ephesians 1:16-23). Later, in 3:6 he says that the mystery he referred to in chapter 1 is that the Gentiles are fellow heirs, members of the same body, and partakers of the promise in Christ Jesus through the gospel. Practically speaking, this new reconciled community is to bear with one another in love, being eager to maintain the unity of the Spirit in the bond of peace. This is because there is one body and one Spirit, one Lord, one faith, one baptism, one God and Father of all, who is over all and through all and in all (Ephesians 4:2-6). In other words, there is one triune God who exists in eternal, diverse, mutually loving, and glorifying community. And this is the image he is bringing to full restoration in humanity through Jesus Christ.

WHY THE NEW NORMAL?

Why was this new normal necessary? Yes, it was God's plan. Yes, it was and is for God's glory. Yes, it was God's original intent that humanity would multiply, fill the earth, and cultivate it in their life of worship together. But sin and the fall resulted in a worship problem. So the new normal became necessary because of our idolatry. In particular, our ethnic identity became a form of our idolatry. We described the events of Acts 2 as the reversal of Babel. God's judgment of humanity at Babel resulted in confusion and separation. As humanity spread out over the earth with separate languages, separate cultures and ethnic identities developed in such a way that differences between people groups became hostile.

Aaron Kuecker, in describing the language of social differentiation, says that ethnicity both in the ancient and modern context "is a powerful expression of the apparently pervasive human impulse toward social categorization and differentiation." He continues by looking at the way Israel saw itself during the New Testament period: "While Israel saw itself as [the people], all non-Israelites populated the out-group [the Gentiles]. The Gentiles constituted the 'them' against which Israelite identity could be forged." Kruecker explains that those deemed Gentiles did not self-identify that way.

As I mentioned in chapter four, our ethnic identity within our people groups *feels* primordial. That is, ethnic identity *feels* absolute, inherent to one's identity. The new normal was necessary to move people to locate their primary identity in Jesus Christ. Doing so helps to guard against making ethnic identity absolute when it is not. Put another way, the new normal of the multiethnic church in the New Testament moves the center of focus to Jesus Christ and finding our identity in him helps avoid cultural idolatry. People's Jewishness was not to be at the center of their identity. People's Egyptian-ness, their Libyan-ness, their Arabian-ness, was not to be at the center of their identity. The Spirit of God worked to press the people of God into the new normal of having Jesus Christ at the center of their identity. As we said at the beginning, this did not mean that ethnic identities were no longer apparent or significant. The work of God was not a call to strike a balance between identity in Christ and ethnic identity, as if too much of one will wash out the other. Instead, those who belonged to Christ were to understand their ethnic identity as subservient to their identity in Christ.

We stand in need of looking back to the new normal of the New Testament church for our way forward in the church today. Christenson, Edwards, and Emerson demonstrate this in their research. Based on their research, they describe the effect of religiously empowered ethnocentrism when it comes to understanding cultural differences saying, "[because] members interpret most of life through a religiously informed grid, differences in culture are often talked about in absolute terms." In our ethnocentric churches, differences in preference get framed in absolute terms. As Miroslav Volf says, both parishioners and clergy are often "trapped within the claims of their own ethnic or cultural community." In other words, our Blackness, our whiteness, our Asian-ness, our Latino-ness still tends to be at the center of our identity even after faith in Jesus Christ!

Only Jesus is able to bear the weight of the center. Your Blackness cannot. Your whiteness cannot. Your American-ness cannot. Your Whatever-ness cannot. God alone has the wisdom, power, and grace to weave the tangled threads of different people, with different cultures, customs, and languages, into a single tapestry of glorious beauty.

The Spirit does not remove our diversity. Rather he enables us to love, hear, seek, understand, and pursue one another *in* our diversity. "With the Holy Spirit, we hear and understand; without him, we misunderstand through fear, distrust, and self-ambition. Unity cannot be engineered; it is a matter of the Spirit."

The fall destroyed union and unity with God and each other. Reunion is the story of Scripture. These words we find throughout God's Word—renewed, reconciled, united—are the reversal of the

Reunion is the story of Scripture.

fractures, divides, breaks, and partitions of life in this world and before God that were and are so desperately needed. We are truly stamped from the beginning for unity and union, for wholeness and shalom, for beauty. God himself is committed to knitting the human race back together in Jesus Christ. This is why, in spite of the inherent instability of the pursuit, in spite of the frustrating feeling of running hard and getting nowhere, we still press on toward the vision.

7

PUT ON YOUR BEAUTIFUL GARMENTS

Culture and Community

In the last chapter, I argued that in order to be in community we have to experience belonging, a sense of being at home. More expressly, belonging is an individual's community experience of being at home among friends as a *co-owner* and *creator* of that community. It includes an individual's sense of being rightly placed in a specific community and feeling welcomed, valued, comfortable, or safe. In a diverse church, however, cultural and ethnic differences confront members often and can hinder belonging.

Melvin brought up the discomfort of relating to others as a Black man in one of Resurrection Church's small group Bible studies. He said, "Mostly their jokes are going over my head. It doesn't give you a good foundation for camaraderie and for fellowship." He certainly wasn't experiencing belonging. However, he chose not to leave the group. He believed that they ought to be like family. In order for that to be the case, they would have to look at culture and understand difference by entering into his whole world, not just his church world. So he invited them to his birthday celebration at a club he described as a "Black-dominated, upper class sort of place." Everyone enjoyed themselves, he said, "but they wouldn't have done that if I had not been in their lives."

When it comes to his diverse church experience, he is clear: "Part of what I see myself as is missional. It's a missional work . . . If I was at a Black church, I wasn't going to be on mission [in this way]." By striving to help people have meaningful experiences with someone they would not normally know, he fostered these relationships and facilitated a sense of belonging. For him, belonging to a crosscultural church means more than exposing others to new ways of thinking or doing. It is an act of leading others to participate in those ways with him.

Darryl and Joyce expressed a similar frustration with their worship experience at their diverse church, All Saints. When I asked them, "What does it feel like to be Black in All Saints church?" Darryl said, "I can't be Black at my church." He continued,

> I mean, the things I would do if I was in a more Black setting, I can't do that. I often suppress it. If I want to worship God, I'm very expressive, and I'm going to express it with my whole being. The culture of All Saints church is pretty much the opposite. If they call me to play the organ, it's a Hammond B organ, but I'm not going to play it the way you would hear it in a Black church. It's the same organ, but it's going to be something they can relate to.

This was a hindrance to belonging for him until he decided to change his perspective in order to experience belonging. "I used to get upset that I would have to suppress [my Blackness], but over time I see [worship] from their perspective." In order for him to have an experience of belonging through worship, he had to change. He had to assimilate. For her part, Joyce struggled with the idea of assimilation. Also a musician at All Saints, she felt the message being communicated to her was, "Not only are you Black, but you can easily assimilate into our culture." She felt as though they were not willing to change to accommodate her. Rather, she was valuable because of her willingness to change and become like them. Darryl and Joyce had different responses to the lack of room made for them in the worship context, but the church's worship culture did not make the experience of belonging easy for either of them.

Dr. Korie Edwards contends that interracial churches in America "remain racially integrated to the extent that they are *first* comfortable places for whites to attend." Those are sobering and uncomfortable words, but they codify the experiences of Melvin, Darryl, and Joyce. Dr. Edwards writes,

> In order to understand the cultural, structural, and social dynamics of interracial churches, race, particularly whiteness, needs to be situated at the heart of the explanation. Given that whiteness is the cornerstone of the racial system in the United States, it plays a fundamental role in how interracial churches function.

Let's be clear—integrated ecclesial communities where whiteness dictates congregational life are not what I mean by beautiful community!

It's necessary to talk about belonging because if we are going to cultivate beautiful community as God's people, there are things that we must commit to doing. Unity cannot be manufactured. It's a matter of the Spirit. And the Spirit of God compels us to pursue this unity in practice. However, to say that we cannot manufacture it is not to say that there's nothing for us to do. We don't just drift our way into beautiful community! The key point here is that for belonging to be real, people have to have a sense of being co-owners and co-creators of the community to which they belong. What does the Bible say to us about the way we put on our beautiful garments together?

> *Unity cannot be manufactured. It's a matter of the Spirit. And the Spirit of God compels us to pursue this unity in practice.*

DRESSED TO IMPRESS

Israel was to be a kingdom of priests and a holy nation (Exodus 19:4-6). Figuratively, they were to dress in holy and beautiful garments like their first high priest, Aaron (Exodus 28:2). This beauty they were to reflect to the nations around them was never fully realized. In Isaiah 51:9 the people of Israel wonder in their distress whether the Lord is sleeping on the job. They cry out,

> Awake, awake, put on strength,
>> O arm of the LORD;
> awake, as in days of old,
>> the generations of long ago.
> Was it not you who cut Rahab in pieces,
>> who pierced the dragon?

They remember the days of old, during the Exodus, when the Lord brought them out with a mighty hand and an outstretched arm. Now, he seems to be asleep and unaware of their predicament. The Lord responds to their cry in Isaiah 52:1,

> Awake, awake,
>> put on your strength, O Zion;
> put on your beautiful garments,
>> O Jerusalem, the holy city;
> for there shall no more come into you
>> the uncircumcised and the unclean.

He isn't the one who was asleep! He calls Zion, his people, to wake up and put on their strength, their beautiful priestly garments as a kingdom of priests. While this is certainly a vision of the future for people of God (Revelation 3:4-5; 21:27), there is a present urgency in the Lord's call for them to put on their beautiful garments. It is a call to live according to who God has declared them to be.

The New Testament picks up on this call to live into our identity as God's people, particularly with the apostle Paul in Colossians 3. In the first verse of the chapter, he says, "If then you have been raised with Christ, seek the things that are above, where Christ is, seated at the right hand of God." Then he tells them in verse 3, "For you all have died and your life is hidden with Christ in God" (author's translation). In Jesus Christ we die. We don't die physically; we die to the power and grip of sin and wickedness over our hearts. Paul says to the Colossians in 2:14 that in Jesus Christ God cancelled the record of debt that stood against us with its legal demands. This he set aside, nailing it to the cross. Therefore, in 2:20, with Christ we died to the elemental spirits of the world. So, when you become a Christian, it's not that you died to die. You died to live! You died, and your *life* is hidden with Christ in God. Now, he is going to tell them what this dying to live looks like in practice.

He says, "Therefore, put to death what is earthly in you . . . You must put them all away (3:5, 8) . . . Here, in the church, there is not Greek and Jew, circumcised and uncircumcised, barbarian, Scythian, slave free, but Christ is all and in all" (v. 11, author's translation). A key question here is, "Will the image of God image God?" When you look at yourself in the mirror, you're not seeing yourself. You're seeing a reflection of yourself. What is most important about the image, its essence, or substance, lies in what it is reflecting. What we find here is Paul pointing out that we were created in the image, according to the likeness of God. When the creation looks at humanity, it should see a reflection of God. Not God himself, but a reflection. The problem, because of sin, is that the mirror is cracked. Not just one little crack. Picture a mirror with cracks

> *In Jesus Christ we die. We don't die physically; we die to the power and grip of sin and wickedness over our hearts.*

throughout, such that when you look at it, you say, "I think I know what that's reflecting, but I'm not too sure." The mirror isn't shattered, but it's badly damaged. Paul is saying that the new self we put on through faith in Christ is being renewed in knowledge after the image of its Creator. The cracks in the mirror are disappearing. But the way that they practically disappear is through brothers and sisters in Christ helping one another to kill the worldly stuff.

The Colossian community to whom Paul is writing included a diverse community of people: Greeks and Jews, circumcised and uncircumcised, barbarians, Scythians, slaves, and free people. The old way includes justifiable divisions based on whatever barriers we prefer. The old way includes staying in our own manufactured lanes, or the lanes we're forced into because of life situations. Slaves can't live like free people. The poor can't hang with the rich. But the new way found in Christ elevates poor people to help rich people drag their idolatrous love for money out into the light and kill it. How can we go further in showing what it means that Christ is all and in all? What are the vestiges of prejudice, pride, or even hatred that remain in us for which we have to cry out to God to remove? Understand that we will never stop having to ask those questions.

You would think that Paul's command to put to death what is earthly (v. 5) would lead him to follow up in verse 12 by simply telling his readers to put on compassionate hearts, kindness, humility, and so on. But he feels compelled to insert a truth statement again. This command is grounded in the fact that those who belong to Christ are God's chosen ones. You are holy. You are loved. Let's take a step back to survey these grounds. To say that this diverse group of people in the Colossian church—Greek, Jew, circumcised, uncircumcised, barbarian, Scythian, slave, free—are God's chosen ones, literally God's elect, is scandalous.

The language of God's chosen has its roots in the Old Testament: "For you are a people holy to the Lord your God. The Lord your God has chosen you to be a people for his treasured possession, out of all the peoples who are on the face of the earth" (Deuteronomy 7:6). This was foundational for Israel's ethnic identity. The truth that the Lord promised their fathers, Abraham, Isaac, and Jacob, that he would make them a great nation, was intricately woven into their sense of who they were as a people. The Lord himself had chosen them out of all the peoples on the face of the earth to be his treasured possession. Understand this, please. We might blow by Paul's words in Colossians 3:12—"God's chosen ones, holy and beloved"—but they were identity shattering words at the time. This was a radically new message delivered at a time before the internet existed. There were no planes, trains, or automobiles. We live in the information age and it still takes a long time for people's views to change. What about a perspective that had been in place for over a thousand years?

This is why Paul's declaration of the grounds for living the Christian life is so incredible. The uncircumcised don't have to become circumcised. The Greek doesn't have to become Jewish. The barbarian isn't excluded because he fails to conform to cultural norms and practices. These boundaries were legitimate reasons people remained separated. What Paul is emphasizing to the Colossians, and by extension to us, is that the starting point for their practice as Christians was the recognition that, in all of their diversity, they stood before God in the same way as Israel. They didn't choose God. He chose them. They weren't holy because they were special and better than everybody else. They were holy because the Lord set his love upon them. Their life was to be grounded in the reality that they were the undeserving recipients of God's abundant love.

Notice Paul's prescription in verse 12 for compassion, kindness, humility, meekness, patience, and forgiveness—these aren't needed when everything is going great. They're needed in the midst of discord. They're needed when controversy looms and understanding runs dry.

They're needed when you've been hurt by somebody in the church, whether they intended to hurt you or not. The love that we're called to dress in as those who follow Jesus Christ is the glue of perfection. That's what Paul says in verse 14. Above everything else, put on love, which binds everything together in perfect harmony. The love we receive from God is impressed on our hearts. It is what enables God's people, who are holy and loved by him, to be tender towards one another in the most trying of times. It's what enables us to ache in our gut for others the way we ache for ourselves when things aren't well.

THE LOOK OF LOVE

If love is the binding glue; if it's expressed in compassion, kindness, humility, meekness, patience, and forgiveness, *especially* when there's unintended hurt; if interracial churches in America default to being places that are comfortable for whites; and if doing so is an actual hindrance to the pursuit of beautiful community, then we have a problem that needs addressing.

Practically speaking, as majority white denominations see the changing ethnic landscape in the United States, they are beginning to understand that their ethnic homogeneity is a hindrance to future growth and sustainability.

The Cooperative Ministries Committee (CMC) of my own denomination, the Presbyterian Church in America (PCA), prepared a strategic plan for the denomination in 2010. The plan sought to address the realities of slowed growth along with a desire to maintain the denomination's "values while honestly facing challenges that could lead to long term decline." It was written to help "the PCA identify its challenges, address them with strategies that are consistent with our biblical values, and build denominational support for implementing these strategies." The report lists the transition from Anglo-majority culture in the United States as an external challenge. Two of the denomination's internal challenges, according to the report, are "maintaining biblical worship with cultural diversity" and "ethnic homogeneity both in general membership and denominational leadership."

Writing on the topic of faith and culture for *Religion News Service* in 2014, Jonathan Merritt asked whether the Southern Baptist Convention (SBC) could thrive in the twenty-first century. He interviewed Dr. David Dockery, then-president of Trinity International University and author of *Southern Baptist Consensus and Renewal: A Biblical, Historical, and Theological Proposal.* In the article Dr. Dockery gave thanks to God for progress in the SBC in the area of racial reconciliation, but added,

> [W]e still have a long way to go in our efforts to live out the kingdom aspirations of diversity and racial reconciliation made known to us in Revelation 7. Thus we need to continue to give much attention to these matters. We need not only focus on what it means to become faithful Great Commission followers of Christ, but also Great Commandment followers of Christ who are called to love those around us.

These denominations continue to wrestle with how to become more ethnically and culturally diverse as a whole, attempting to discover what it looks like to love those around them. David Livermore explains this challenge when he says, "We have to learn to *be* the people who become culturally accessible, living messages of Jesus and his love. Embodying Jesus crossculturally is a messy, complicated process. This is what often splits churches, divides families, and erodes Christian fellowship." My primary concern is not to help white denominations or churches answer the question about the practical problem around the changing ethnic landscape of America. My practical concern is to address the pursuit of beautiful community, putting on the binding glue of love.

Chapter 26 of the Westminster Confession of Faith, "Of the Communion of Saints," is a verbal portrait of what this love looks like. The authors of the 1646 document (the Westminster Divines) examined the Scriptures and came to a consensus on the Christian obligation to love one another (Romans 13:8). Since we are united to one another in love we have communion in each other's gifts and graces. This union obligates us to pursue the things that lead to our mutual good. And not just in nonmaterial ways. But it's the "public and private" mutual good of "the inward and outward man." That means every kind of spiritual need, emotional, physical, monetary, and so on. This mutual good is further described as mutual edification, the building up of one another. And as God provides opportunity, this communion, or covenant love, is to be extended to all those in every place who call on the name of the Lord Jesus.

It is important to note that our resources are spiritual. Whether those resources are nonmaterial or material, they are spiritual at heart. This is an important distinction. When I say that the church's resources are spiritual, I mean that her resources have to do with the power and work of the Spirit of God. Her resources are spiritual because her aim is the glory of God and the flourishing of her neighbors. The question is not whether someone needs spiritual care or physical care. No. We all need spiritual care. The question is what type of spiritual care is required?

The communion of the saints and the obligation to love are, of course, rooted in the trinitarian foundation we laid in part one of this book. Robert Letham rightly points out that the joy of Christian fellowship is an outflow of trinitarian doctrine. Yet, this communion does not negate or diminish the integrity of the individual. Christian unity and union is in diversity. Like the mutuality in the Trinity, the first paragraph of chapter 26 in the Westminster Confession expresses mutuality for Christian community. Professor and author Chad Van Dixhoorn, commenting on the Confession's statement, remarks, "Ultimately this love for each other cannot be restricted to what we have; it needs to encompass who we are." He is calling for a Christian identity of mutual love in community. R. C. Sproul, reflecting on the Confession, implies agreement by saying that the ingredient which makes the communion of the saints cohesive is love. William Perkins, one of the Westminster Divines, explained centuries before the other men referenced here that Christian community shares mutual love expressed in mutual obligation: "We must here be admonished not to seek our own things, but to refer the labours of our callings to the common good . . . Lastly, considering we are all knit into one mystical body . . . our duty is to redress the faults of our brethren, and to cover them . . . Love covers the multitude of sins." A generation ago, Princeton Seminary Professor George S. Hendry explained this love as not being based on mutual attraction. "Rather, it is a love that overcomes division and reconciles contraries, bringing into communion those who have nothing in common except the fact that Christ gave himself for them."

In God, as we have seen, there is unity in diversity, diversity in unity. As Herman Bavinck wrote about the unity of God, "Among us unity exists only by attraction, by the will and the disposition of the will; it is a moral unity that is fragile and unstable." In the normal course of human relationships, unity is primarily based on mutual attraction. This is true in everything from marriages to sports teams. Yet, they are fragile and unstable. The team that wins the Super Bowl this year will talk about their unity in interviews. They'll describe the ways in which they have been on the same page since training camp, aligned together for the same purpose. However, the team who takes the field next year will have the same uniforms, but they'll have to recreate their unity. There will be new team members and new challenges. And there's no guarantee that their attempts at unity will be successful. In fact, in all likelihood, they won't be.

This is why Hendry's explanation of the communion of the saints is profound. The particular expression of love that the world should see when it looks at Jesus' church is the evident overcoming of divisions. It is the evidence that contraries have been reconciled. It is the expression of love that belies a normally fragile and unstable unity. It is the outworking of an abnormal love, one not based on mutual attraction. The common denominator in Christian love is that Jesus gave himself for us. We will spend the rest of this book fleshing out the way we put on our beautiful garments. We cultivate beautiful community in the way we Devote to the Doctrine, Probe the Preferences, Count the Cost, and Toast to the Truth.

> *The common denominator in Christian love is that Jesus gave himself for us.*

8

HOW BEAUTIFUL ARE THE FEET

Gospel Message—Devote to the Doctrine

Patrick immigrated to America from the Democratic Republic of Congo. He's a member of a diverse church in a midwestern city. I asked him to tell me about a time when he could describe his experience at church as, "I'm home here. I'm theirs and they're mine." He said, "I always tell my wife that we don't have to pretend to be Christian. We are Christian. So, if we go to church, we are not going to see what jacket the pastor is wearing today. We are going to listen to the Word of God. And what sticks to me in this church is the message I get from the pastor. That's really what makes me love this church, the message. The way they preach. That's what we need as Christians. That's our food, our daily meal, you know?"

Dinesh is a member of a diverse church in a mid-Atlantic city. When I asked him to describe the impact his church community had on him, he said, "The great thing that I see is the gospel working; the power of the gospel working in me and in other people. And I see how sin has affected humanity. In each culture it does it differently. And God is in the business of redeeming that. And that's what's amazing to me."

Eun, a member of a diverse church in yet another city, said she wasn't necessarily looking for a diverse church to join. The issue for her centered around the church's message. In her search, she asked the question, "Is the pastor preaching the gospel, and am I going to get fed?"

In spite of her struggles at All Saints, Joyce, who we met earlier in this book, realized that if she chose to go to a different church it would boil down to her preferences and "not because of things that are truly essential, like the teaching of God's Word."

Alea did not initially feel an overwhelming sense of welcome at Cross Community Church. When asked why she continued to make the over one-hour drive to church each week she said, "I had never really heard truth the way it was shared here."

One of the common threads I found throughout my research of diverse churches was that participants placed a high importance on each church's commitment to God's Word and doctrinal soundness. People were willing to overlook or work through the difficulties of being in a diverse church if that church was committed to the Bible as its central authority. How do we put on our beautiful garment of love as God's people? The first necessity is to devote to the doctrine.

By "devote to the doctrine" I mean that churches need to embrace the theology of unity in diversity as a gospel imperative. The one God eternally exists in three persons. The three persons are distinct (thus, diverse) and are perfectly united in being and action. His unity in diversity as beautiful community is instructive for how he designed humanity to image him. Therefore, we should not be surprised to see the Bible express unity in diversity from Adam and Eve in Genesis to every people and nation in Revelation. Thus, in the church there are many members yet one body. And the Bible indicates that God intends for his church to represent humanity's diversity. This diversity is not just a generalization for a worldwide body, but a specific reality for individual churches in local communities.

The gospel imperative for the church is not simply the call to a personal relationship with God through Jesus Christ. In that way of expressing the gospel message, a radically individualistic emphasis overwhelms the definition of what it means to be a Christian. While no one would argue against the idea that the Lord saves individuals and reconciles them to himself, the gospel is so much more than that. It must include the fulness of what it means to be made in the image of God. The finished image, the most telling and striking likeness of God, is the entirety of redeemed humanity.

The prophet Isaiah connects beauty to the gospel when he writes, "How beautiful upon the mountains are the feet of him who brings good news, who publishes peace, who brings good news of happiness, who publishes salvation, who says to Zion, 'Your God reigns'" (Isaiah 52:7). The good news is the victory of God. The victory of God that accomplishes peace, happiness, and salvation for a fragmented and sinful humanity. To quote Peter Leithart again,

> *The gospel imperative for the church is not simply the call to a personal relationship with God through Jesus Christ.*

> The good news is the good news of the unity of the human race. And the Church is a proleptic sign of that eschatological reality. It is a sign of the unity of the human race that will one day be perfectly achieved. It is also a sign of a cosmic unity that all things are summed up in Christ, and the Church is to be the visible communion of human beings that anticipates that ultimate union of all things in Christ. It is a living sign; a community where that unity is already experienced in some degree. . . . This, in some respects, is the whole point of redemptive history. That God is going to knit back the human race in his Son. When the Church fails to be that proleptic reality of the eschatological union of all things in Christ, then we are very deeply failing in the calling we've been given.

For the church to be a proleptic sign is for it to function as a forward-facing mirror. People should look at the church and get a glimpse of where the world is heading.

Holding a position like this will change the character of preaching in a church as well as the way it lives in fellowship. It will militate against the truncated Great Commission Christianity described by Dr. Bradley. Cultivating beautiful community by devoting ourselves to the doctrine of unity in diversity as a gospel imperative will compel us to press into issues of justice, racism, and oppression. We will embrace the gospel call for repentance where we've dishonored our Lord Jesus Christ by becoming opponents of injustice, racism, and oppression. We will also embrace the gospel call to repair and restore as fruit of our repentance.

DEVOTING TO THE DOCTRINE

What I am saying here is nothing novel. It's not a radical approach to living out the implications of our faith. Devotion to the doctrine is simply a plea for the church to reject an idolatrous spirituality of the church. To be clear, the church's mission and resources are spiritual at heart. This is true whether we are talking about material or non-material matters. To say that the mission is spiritual is to say that it has to do with the power and work of the Spirit of God. To say that her resources are spiritual is to say that her aim is the glory of God and the flourishing of her neighbors. An idolatrous spirituality, on the other hand, makes an unbiblical distinction between the material and non-material aspects of life. It is an unhealthy approach to the faith that separates the gospel from social impact and engagement by overly spiritualizing it. Warning against such an approach, the apostle James asks a set of rhetorical questions:

> What good is it, my brothers, if someone says he has faith but does not have works? Can that faith save him? If a brother or sister is poorly clothed and lacking in daily food, and one of you says to them, "Go in peace, be warm and filled," without giving them the things needed for the body, what good is that? So also faith by itself, if it does not have works, is dead. (James 2:14-17)

What good is it? It's no good to make a false dichotomy between the spiritual and the material. Well-wishing is not enough when the church encounters real needs that have an impact on the well-being of image-bearers. We saw this expressed in chapter 26 of the Westminster Confession of Faith where Christian love is expressed as an obligation to do what makes for the mutual good of one another inwardly and outwardly, publicly and privately. But if we really devote to the doctrine of unity in diversity it gets even more nuanced than that.

Let me again utilize the confessional commitment of my own tradition to emphasize that what I am saying is neither novel nor radical in Protestantism. Presbyterians assert that the Westminster Confession of Faith, together with its Larger and Shorter Catechisms, is a faithful representation of the system of doctrine taught in Scripture. The Larger Catechism (WLC) comprises 196 questions covering what we are to believe as well as the duties God requires of us. The purpose of a catechism is instruction. And, in this case, it is instruction for those who have received some introduction to Christianity. Question 93 begins an important section on the Ten Commandments and its implications for us:

Q. 93. What is the moral law?

A. The moral law is the declaration of the will of God to mankind, directing and binding every one to personal, perfect, and perpetual conformity and obedience thereunto, in the frame and disposition of the whole man, soul and body, and in performance of all those duties of holiness and righteousness which he oweth to God and man: promising life upon the fulfilling, and threatening death upon the breach of it.

God's moral law is the declaration of his will, and everyone—the religious and irreligious, young and old, rich and poor, male and female, Black and white—is bound to obey it. Then, question 98 asks where the moral law is summarily comprehended. The answer? The Ten Commandments. The first four commandments express our duty to God while the remaining six express our duty to humanity, to our neighbors. The Catechism rightly understands that the commandments do not simply forbid sin, telling us what not to do. But where a sin is forbidden, the opposite duty is required. In other words, when the sixth commandment says, "You shall not murder" (Exodus 20:13), it's not enough to refrain from killing somebody. To obey the commandment, we have to be people who promote and preserve life.

In our focus on devoting to the doctrine, I want to look briefly at commandments five and six. The fifth commandment says, "Honor your father and your mother, that your days may be long in the land the LORD your God is giving you" (20:12). WLC question and answer 124 explains that our natural parents are not the only ones in view here, "but all superiors in age and gifts; and especially such as, by God's ordinance, are over us in place of authority, whether in family, church, or commonwealth." God calls us to honor all legitimate authority (Romans 13:1-7). But he also requires those in authority to act in a certain way with regard to those under their authority.

WLC question 129 asks, "What is required of superiors towards their inferiors?" Question 130 asks, "What are the sins of superiors?" The answers tell us that those in authority are to love, pray for, and bless those under their authority. They are to protect those in their care and provide for them all things necessary for soul and body. However, those in authority sin when they exercise their authority in a way that leads to their own glory, ease, profit, or pleasure and command things that are unlawful, or not in the power of those under their authority to perform.

When the state fails to do its duty to administer public justice, when it does not enact and enforce just and equitable laws that promote public welfare, how can it know that it stands in violation of the moral law of God? How will the civil authorities know they are out of accord with their duty to God? The civil government, as an institution, does not base its governance and oversight on a robust understanding of what the Lord says about goodness, justice, and righteousness. Johannes G. Vos, in his commentary on this part of the WLC, writes,

> As for the state, its obligation consists chiefly in protecting and upholding the freedom and security of the individual, the family, and the church, and in administering public justice, enacting and enforcing just and equitable laws, and providing for the public welfare in times of crisis or emergency.

Here's the point: If the church is not willing to speak up and call the civil government to account, other voices will fill that void. You see, our desire as the church ought not be to create a theocracy in whatever nation we reside. But it most certainly ought to be seeing public justice administered well. This is something that the Black church in America has understood by necessity. Those within its ranks have not been the carriers of social and political gravitas. Having existed for most of American history as a marginalized minority with limited to no agency in the culture forced the Black church to adopt this right understanding of our duty to speak out against injustice in the public square. The majority white church, on the other hand, has enjoyed the luxury of neglecting public justice as a part of the church's calling.

What does devotion to this doctrine have to do with cultivating beautiful community? Those on the receiving end of public injustice in America have historically been black and brown people. We can no longer talk about unity in diversity while simultaneously refusing to consciously address the public justice issues that still have an impact on people of color. As I said, this is not

If the church is not willing to speak up and call the civil government to account, other voices will fill that void.

radical. It's simply being willing to live like we believe what we confess. Most of the diverse churches I engaged in my research put issues of race and justice front and center as a way of facilitating the experience of belonging. They held forums and conferences that provided a space for people to experience vulnerability in themselves and others.

Eun described an occasion at church when, during a Q&A, a Black woman stood up to speak. Rather than asking a question, the woman rose to apologize for thinking a certain way about race. This shocked Eun. She said, "For her to feel so comfortable and safe to talk about herself that way, I was just shocked. I was like, 'This [church] is different.'" Joyce was grateful for her church's willingness to bring up the issues of race and invite open dialogue. One moment that stood out to her concerned when a woman of color shared a thought that people of color in the room received well whereas the white people reacted to it poorly. She called it a teaching and learning moment that opened up other areas of the conversation "that were probably hidden before that, and that no one would have ever really discussed." Opening up to dialogue about race can facilitate belonging in a powerful way amidst the challenges it may bring.

At the same time, it is worth noting that belonging can be hindered in this same type of context. Melvin expressed hurt when he recalled no one at his church asking how the shooting death of Michael Brown affected him. "I was so devastated," he said. Their silence caused him to wonder whether they knew him well at all. He thought to himself, "You don't know my history and my background; how I think about the police. You're just making assumptions."

Each of these examples comes from internal forums and conversations in churches on issues of race and justice. Devoting to the doctrine of unity in diversity means engaging the difficult issues faced in the public square, but it starts with an internal engagement in the church.

The same kind of commitment is laid out for us in the sixth commandment, "You shall not murder." It is sobering to consider what this commandment requires of us. To not murder includes actively resisting whatever strips life unjustly. So, the sins forbidden in the commandment include neglecting or withdrawing the necessary means for preserving life.

The Westminster Divines were certainly influenced by John Calvin's explication of the sixth commandment in *The Institutes of the Christian Religion*. He wrote,

> The purport of this commandment is, that since the Lord has bound the whole human race by a kind of unity, the safety of all ought to be considered as entrusted to each. In general, therefore, all violence and injustice, and every kind of harm from which our neighbor's body suffers, is prohibited. Accordingly, we are required faithfully to do what in us lies to defend the life of our neighbor, to promote whatever tends to his tranquility, to be vigilant in warding off harm, and, when danger comes, to assist in removing it.

It is essential for us to keep driving home the truth that every institution and person is bound by God to this duty of preserving life and must avoid taking away the necessary means for doing so. So, the church rightly engages the topic of abortion in the public square. God's people ought to be pro-life. The question is are we pro-life enough? As I said earlier, every person, from the womb to the tomb, has a beauty and a value that is independent of our abilities and what we produce. Has the church in America taken seriously enough the obligation to speak into what is necessary for the promotion, preservation, and flourishing of human life from the womb to the tomb, especially when it comes to the lives of those who are on the margins and underrepresented in positions of power?

The implications of the sixth commandment touch on education. They extend to health care, housing, employment, and wages. It is the same doctrinal commitment that caused Black Presbyterian clergy in

American history to advocate in the public arena for the well-being of people of color.

Samuel Eli Cornish was the "first black man to undergo the normal exacting training and testing procedures required for Presbyterian ordination." In 1824 Pastor Cornish started the first Black Presbyterian church in New York City. He was also an abolitionist. He launched the first Black newspaper, *Freedom's Journal*, along with two other papers, *Rights of All* and *The Colored American*.

Pastor Theodore Wright helped to start the American Anti-Slavery Society in 1833.

Pastor J. C. Pennington helped raise money and seek justice for the fugitives of the Amistad.

In 1880 Pastor Matthew Anderson planted Berean Presbyterian Church in Philadelphia, which launched a number of sixth commandment related ministry initiatives, including a savings bank, a building and loan association, a manual training school, a medical dispensary, and a kindergarten. When he went to plant the church among "the colored people of Philadelphia," he drew some conclusions along the way as to the hindrances and opportunities that lay before him. Two in particular are worth highlighting:

> The apathy of the Presbytery had to be overcome by arousing them to the importance of the work. Mission work had so long been neglected among the colored people that the Presbyteries had almost lost sight of them, and they were very ignorant as to their real wants and condition.

> The apathy of the colored people also had to be overcome. In saying that we saw a demand for the establishment of a Presbyterian Church among the colored people, we do not for a moment mean to imply that they were anxious and eager to have a church planted among them and were standing ready to do all in their

power to sustain it, not by any means . . . There was a demand for the church, but . . . it was demanded by the condition and wants of the colored people. They themselves, were for the most part indifferent, . . . not so much toward the establishment of this particular church, but towards the Presbyterian Church generally, and this prejudice was inherited, being associated in their minds with the church which encouraged slavery, also as being cold, aristocratic, pharisaical, and which had no use for the Negro more than to use him as a servant. This spirit would have to be overcome before there would be any marked success.

Here, Reverend Anderson calls out two things: the apathy of the white Presbytery and their lack of concern for the full life of the Black people in their area. He's planting his church because, in my words, his white brethren are not willing to live into their doctrinal and confessional commitment. Secondly, their unwillingness has not gone unnoticed by the Black community. They were well aware of this lack of care.

Reverend Francis J. Grimké pastored Fifteenth Street Presbyterian Church in Washington, DC for fifty years (1878–1928). Grimké helped form the Niagara Movement and the National Association for the Advancement of Colored People (NAACP). He also assisted in forming the American Negro Academy. In his pastorate he labored at presenting to people, in word and deed, the Lord Jesus Christ and their need for his saving power. Because of that he also said, "I have always been ready to speak in behalf of the rights of the race, and have never hesitated to condemn, and in the strongest terms, those who are trying to deprive us of our rights as men and as American citizens."

These Black Presbyterian ministers understood the implications of their confessional commitment. In contrast, white evangelical churches formed private Christian schools to keep their children from having to attend school with Black children during the desegregation of public schools. In the Black church tradition, where schools were formed (including tutoring programs), they were formed as a sixth commandment issue to promote life and flourishing for Black children. They were formed because the civil authorities refused to do what was necessary for the flourishing of Black children. They were formed so that Black children would understand that their lives matter too.

DESCRIPTION NOT PRESCRIPTION

We could go on further exploring the way our doctrinal commitments expressed in commandments seven, eight, nine, and ten lay a foundation for pursuing beautiful community. I pray that my brief sketch here is enough to demonstrate how a robust doctrinal devotion influences the preaching ministry, communal life, and civic engagement of the church. I am not giving you a prescription to follow, but a description of what to consider as we cultivate beautiful community. The power Jesus Christ has given the church is only ministerial and declarative. As his ministers and ambassadors, we declare to each other, our neighbors, our communities, and our world what the Lord says. We do it for the purpose of building up and pursuing the common good.

The way in which we declare his Word matters, but it is also varied. Devoting to the doctrine necessitates our finding ways to faithfully bring God's Word to bear in our diverse communities such that it has an effect on the circumstances of the whole person. It means that our doctrinal commitment will tangibly demonstrate that we care about the systemic impact of sin upon our neighbors. We won't truncate the gospel message as if it only addresses personal sin and brokenness. We will address the systems and structures in the public and ecclesial arenas that deny our neighbors their inherent dignity as image-bearers.

9

THE BEAUTY
OF HOLINESS

Probe the Preferences and Count the Cost

Ascribe to the LORD, O families of the peoples,
ascribe to the LORD glory and strength!
Ascribe to the LORD the glory due his name;
bring an offering, and come into his courts!
Worship the LORD in the splendor of holiness;
tremble before him, all the earth!

PSALM 96:7-9

I n **November 2013,** *The Washington Post* published an article on the rise of super zip codes in America. Super Zips are the zip codes ranking highest on income and college education. The largest collection of Super Zips, according to the article, appears around Washington, DC, with the affluent becoming more isolated from the working class and the poor. Demonstrating our preference for sameness the authors state that, "Many Washington neighborhoods are becoming more economically homogenous as longtime homeowners move out and increasing housing prices prevent the less affluent from moving in." Robert Putnam writes, "More and more families live either in uniformly affluent neighborhoods or in uniformly poor neighborhoods . . . While race-based segregation has been slowly declining, class-based segregation has been increasing." Putnam specifically laments the social stratification of his childhood city, Port Clinton, Ohio. At one time, the city's distribution of income was among the most egalitarian in the country. Now, the Lake Erie shore in Port Clinton is lined with elaborate mansions and gated communities "almost uninterruptedly for 20 miles on either side of town . . . and it is possible to walk in less than ten minutes from wealthy estates on the shoreline to impoverished trailer parks inland."

Regarding the church Glenn Bracey and Wendy Moore write,

An uneasy tension exists between two common perceptions of American society. It is axiomatic that American churches are voluntary associations, where those with doctrinal affinity are free to participate or not, without any forms of official coercion (Warner 1993). Yet, the membership of nearly 90 percent of American congregations is at least 90 percent of the same race (Emerson and Kim 2003). In other words, although predominantly white churches are more diverse than twenty years ago, the Church remains extremely racially segregated (Chaves 2011:29–32).

In contemporary American society and the church, our preference for sameness is still very real.

In 1954 psychologist Gordon Allport, often called a founding father of personality psychology, described this phenomenon with the term *in-group*. Members of an in-group "use the term *we* with the same essential significance." The preference for sameness is also positive. Allport argues that in-group memberships are vitally important to individual survival. When in-group members encounter an outsider with different customs, they realize that the outsider has different habits, which the in-group receives as habit-breaking. Because the familiar is preferred, habit-breaking is unpleasant.

This preference for in-group sameness is often unconscious. In their research, Christian Smith and Michael Emerson demonstrate the unconscious nature of this preference. By studying racialization in America, they found that highly educated whites are less likely to say that they are uncomfortable with Black neighbors when compared to less well-educated whites. The research also showed that in spite of what these highly educated whites say, they are, in actuality, more segregated from Black Americans than are whites with less education. As a result, their children are more likely to attend racially homogenous schools. Their lives demonstrated an unconscious preference for sameness that contradicted their words.

The shaping and transforming effect of culture includes learned behaviors, ideas that reinforce beliefs and values, and products that reinforce beliefs. If we're going to love crossculturally, we have to become crosscultural people. However, our preference for sameness in groups exacerbates the challenge of doing so. One of culture's influences on our identity formation is in providing a means to differentiate between one group and another, and a corresponding desire to maintain group sameness. This preference for sameness may be cultural, ethnic, or socioeconomic, among other things. Putnam claims that when it comes to social capital, "Individuals form connections that benefit our own interests."

We have already talked at length about ghettoization in society and in the church. In Psalm 96, the psalmist calls the families of the peoples to ascribe to the Lord the glory and strength that he is due, commanding the nations to worship him in the beauty of his holiness. The

> *If we're going to love crossculturally, we have to become crosscultural people.*

vision here is one of the nations coming into the courts of the temple in holy attire. Some English translations render the Hebrew of verse 9, "Worship the Lord in holy attire." It is another instance in which the Bible calls us away from our ghettoization into united worship of God in our diversity, dressed in beautiful attire.

How do we find our way out of sinful ghettoization? If the first step is to devote to the doctrine, the second is to probe our preferences. It is essential to probe our preferences in the pursuit of beautiful community because we cannot ignore the fact that there is a positive aspect of in-group membership. As we cultivate beautiful community, we are being shaped and formed into a new in-group and, as Allport said, members of an in-group use the term *we* with the same essential significance. So, beautiful community is the crafting of a new *we*. This is not a call for people to forget or become less aware of their ethnicity. Rather, it is a call to embrace their identity as part of a new group. For this to take place, we need to probe the cultural preferences of our ghettos that hinder the formation of a new *we*.

Even as churches strive to be faithful to the Lord, that faithfulness is often necessarily expressed through preferences. The Bible simply does not tell us every detail of every aspect of a worship service or daily life. Some things we have to figure out by "good and necessary consequence" of what the Bible does say. How often do churches probe their preferences to find out whether they help or hinder diverse people from experiencing welcome? Our preferences are based on cultural values that lie beneath the surface of the things we see, hear, and experience. Although churches are formed by those values, they are often assumed and go unaddressed. Therefore, churches need to develop an awareness of the unseen cultural values among them. If they are to pursue the creation of a new *we*, where the dividing walls of hostility are broken down, they cannot afford to ignore the values that form their expression of church.

PROBING THE PREFERENCES

You would be hard-pressed to find a church that openly says, "We don't believe in hospitality here. We're not interested in welcoming people who differ from us." Hospitality is a key practice in cultivating beautiful community. But Soong-Chan Rah helpfully lays out the difficulty to hospitality in a crosscultural context.

> A newcomer to a church might ask, "Do I belong here? Is there a place for me?" If the spectrum of experience is limited to one particular frame of cultural reference, the newcomer does not feel welcomed because his or her frame of reference is outside the cultural norms and boundaries of that church.

He asks further, "What type of hospitality does your church extend toward those who are coming from different cultural contexts so they feel welcomed and part of the proceedings?" These questions are important because, as Christine Pohl points out, communities in which hospitality is a vibrant practice tap into deep human longings for belonging and value. Hospitable communities recognize that they are incomplete without other people, and they believe that others have a treasure to share with their community.

Research shows that turnover rates within religious organizations are higher for minority groups than for majority groups. Christerson, Edwards, and Emerson differentiated core members from edge members in each religious organization they studied, edge members being those who are atypical to the organization. Core members are those who belong to the largest group, the group having the most influence and power while sharing a visceral connection with the identity and mission of the organization. While edge people experienced a continual pull to leave the organization, hospitality

Hospitality is a key practice in cultivating beautiful community.

drew them toward the core. In Miroslav Volf's view, making space for others and inviting them in—even enemies—is an imperative for those who have been embraced by God.

The primary question we must ask when probing our preferences is, "Why do we do the things we do in the way that we do them?" I am privileged to have frequent opportunities to preach and speak at a variety of churches across the country. In most, even the ones that are statistically diverse, whites make up the majority. Typically, the people of color in these churches want to meet with me for a time of fellowship and conversation while I am in town. They want to talk about the challenges of navigating life as ethnic minorities in a majority white church context. For different reasons they feel called to their church and embrace a life of unity in diversity. Yet, they struggle. I always ask some form of this question, "What does it cost you to be here?" I want to hear their story. Invariably, they respond that no one at church has ever asked them a question like this. The church typically assumes that it's welcoming and remains painfully unaware of the cost paid by minorities to be a part of their communion. One young African American man said that his family wanted to know what he was doing at that white church. Another young African American man said his grandmother's response was, "Don't worry baby. When they turn their backs on you, we'll still be here." The answers are not always that stark, but the issue of trust is prominent. Branson and Martinez put it this way,

> Our capacities to understand each other, to share in work, and to hope require an increasing consciousness about our own worldviews and a commitment to listen and walk under the influence of the worldviews of others. For many in the dominant culture, in which one element of the lifeworld is entitlement, this can be a stressful experience. For those in the minority the need for trust remains a challenge, especially if memories are saturated with wounds.

The goal of probing our preferences for deeper cultural self-awareness is not to remove the experience of difficulty in diverse churches. That would be impossible. Rather, it is to impress upon diverse churches that if they want to help facilitate belonging through hospitality and contribute to the healthy formation of a new *we*, they must be aware of the values that underlie their practices and how those practices are received by others.

Those in the minority are more aware of the underlying cultural values in the community because they experience their impact more directly. Let me tell you what people of color typically do in that context: They adopt a mission mindset. They take on a missional approach to educating the majority culture people in their church. They begin to see their membership as God's call to help educate other church members who have not developed any substantive relationships with people from their ethnic group.

For example, Eun realized that people have all kinds of preconceived notions about Korean American culture. She said that discussions about food are typically pleasant until someone asks an insensitive question such as, "Do Korean people actually eat dog?" For her, getting angry only perpetuates ignorance. Instead, she responds with a gracious attitude that says, "It's really annoying, but let me just school you, let me just educate you." Indeed, she said she loves how God is using her to spread the knowledge of Korean people to her church.

Likewise, Joyce embraced the educational aspect of belonging at her church. Although she struggled with feeling like a token, she realized that people looked to her and other Blacks in the congregation as a gauge for how to interact with other people of color. She said, "You're almost like an image, or you're like a display to educate people." If this feeling of being on display to educate people were taking place on her job, she would not embrace it. But she does so at her church as a way of experiencing belonging because she finds herself among her brothers and sisters in Christ, with whom she sees herself growing. Andrea, a Black female member of Living Hope, has embraced her role as an ethnic minority to "raise the consciousness of the group." She said, "It's very unique. It gives you a way to introduce aspects of your culture and what you've come from to folks who, without this relationship, might not engage in that fully."

Churches must probe their preferences because, for ethnic minorities, the missional mindset can run its course and begin to work against the experience of belonging. People regularly expressed to me feelings of "minority fatigue." The missional mindset will run its course if minorities are the only ones doing all of the adjusting.

How do you probe the preferences given these challenges? There are two actions I want to emphasize. The first is prayer. Your corporate heart has to be in the right place. Prayer is primary because God is real. The testimony of the Bible is that God's people pray without ceasing. We praise when things are going well, and we plead in times of need. Probing preferences is about heart examination.

It is common for pastors to quote from 1 Corinthians 11:23-29 in preparing the church to eat the Lord's Supper. Congregants grow accustomed to hearing, "Let a person examine himself, then, and so eat of the bread and drink of the cup" (11:28). The context of this passage concerns divisions in the Corinthian church that Paul needs to address (11:18). These sinful divisions are put on display in their table fellowship. They don't share as they ought. Some eat and drink to excess while others go hungry. Paul says this kind of behavior humiliates those who have nothing and evidences that they despise the church of God! What is the appropriate response? An examination of the heart to discern whether or not they really grasp the implications of the reconciling and reunifying gospel of Jesus Christ.

This need extends beyond the Lord's Supper to every aspect of the church's life where we fail to demonstrate a robust grasp of the reconciling power of Jesus Christ. So often, we don't know what we don't know. We are regularly blind to the ways we maintain boundaries in the body of Christ that our Savior destroyed when he rose from the dead and ascended to the right hand of the majesty on high. We might be blind, but the Spirit of God is not!

So, we need to believe Jesus when he says to us, "Ask, and it will be given to you; seek, and you will find; knock, and it will be opened to you. . . . If you then, who are evil, know how to give good gifts to your children, how much more will your Father who is in heaven give good things to those who ask him!" (Matthew 7:7, 11). It takes prayer to probe our preferences because much of what we find will be painful, difficult, and require humility.

My second recommended action follows on this point. Get outside help! You need someone from the outside to help you see what you can't see and to create a context for people who are a part of the church share their painful experiences. Here's where a tool like the Intercultural Development Inventory (IDI) can be extremely helpful. When I come alongside churches, ministries and organizations I utilize the IDI as a way of helping them probe their preferences. I call the IDI a common grace tool. It wasn't developed to help the church in particular, but it is currently the premier crosscultural assessment of intercultural competence. When we imagine a culture, we should have the image of an iceberg in view. Above the surface of the water are the artifacts, products, and institutions of a culture. They compose the aspects of culture we experience with our five senses and include things like dress, food, art, literature, language, music, games, and holidays. However, ships have wrecked because they mistakenly thought most of the iceberg was comprised of what their eyes could see. In the same way, our crosscultural efforts wreck when we engage primarily at a surface level in our attempts to step across lines of difference. Like an iceberg, most of a culture's life is unseen. In fact, the products of a culture form from the values that lay beneath the surface of the water. There we find values, beliefs, social expectations, parenting styles, gender roles, ideas of modesty, concepts of time, importance of space, the nature of friendship, concepts of beauty, and other unspoken aspects of culture that shape our understanding of who we are. As a reminder, it is these reinforced behaviors and ideas that are the true barriers to beautiful community because of our ghettoization.

The IDI calls the artifacts, products, and institutions above the surface of the water objective culture. It describes the values, beliefs, and behaviors below the surface subjective culture. The IDI helps answer the question, "What is going on with us internally when we experience difference?" It measures the degree of subjective culture competence across a development continuum extending from mono-cultural mindsets to intercultural mindsets. The benefit of this tool is that it provides a benchmark for churches, giving them a tangible grasp of how hospitable they really are for diverse peoples. Most receive no formal training on becoming interculturally competent so it should be no surprise that most of us substantially overestimate our intercultural capability!

The IDI will tell you where you perceive yourself along the inter-cultural development continuum. It will also tell you where you actually are on the continuum and help you understand the gap between your perception and reality. This is a humbling process for most people. And while the IDI is not the inerrant, inspired, infallible Word of God, it sets the table for helpful conversations and for preferences to be probed by affirming the need for probing if they're going to grow into beautiful community. Minority members in majority culture churches are given a framework to express the accommodations they've had to make to be a part of the community. Majority culture members begin to learn about their own unseen and assumed preferences.

COUNTING THE COST

In probing the preferences churches ask questions like:

"What is the history of our church?"

"What drives the content of our Sunday morning liturgy?"

"What value do we place on music?"

It asks these kinds of questions to discern whether it's serious about the desire for beautiful community in its expression of life together. Or is it simply after a multicolored but mono-cultural life? Is it only interested in different hues in the pews? If beautiful community is the desired pursuit, then how should the Sunday morning liturgy change to communicate welcome to a church's diverse neighbors? What sermon application points speak to the core cultural concerns of a church's diverse neighbors? What community life practices are inviting to a church's diverse neighbors? In what ways does a church need to listen and learn from its diverse neighbors in order to grow while also making disciples?

All of this is a part of probing our preferences, but it is not the end. If churches desire to grow into beautiful community, they have to count the cost. Salvation is free, but it's not cheap. Our salvation cost Jesus his life, and it costs us ours. Jesus says that if we're going to follow him, we need to be like a builder who's about to take on a construction project. The builder doesn't launch into the project thoughtlessly, but first sits down and counts the cost asking, "Do I have enough time, materials and money to complete this project" (Luke 14:26-28)? We have to count the cost of being his disciples. Similarly, cultivating beautiful community is not cheap because it is also about discipleship. It will cost you preferences. To put it another way, you will, by necessity, have to die to self for the sake of extending grace to your diverse neighbors. The cultivation of

> *Salvation is free, but it's not cheap. Our salvation cost Jesus his life, and it costs us ours.*

beautiful community is a cruciform pursuit. What preferences do we have that have morphed into idols that need to be destroyed? What preferences do we need to loosen our grip on?

In Romans 15:1-7 we see that counting the cost of cultivating beautiful community is an aspect of discipleship. We don't find the words *beautiful* or *community* in those verses, but that's what Paul describes when he prays, "May the God of endurance and encouragement grant you to live in such harmony with one another, in accord with Christ Jesus, that together you may with one voice glorify the God and Father of our Lord Jesus Christ. Therefore welcome one another as Christ has welcomed you, for the glory of God" (vv. 5-7).

The apostle is talking about beautiful community as a way of life, and he begins the chapter addressing the way we count the cost. He says in verses 1-2, "But we who are strong have an obligation to bear the weaknesses of those without strength, and not to please ourselves. Let each of us please his neighbor for good, to build him up" (author's translation). The weak he's talking about here are those weak in faith, as described in Romans 14. Their weakness is demonstrated by the fact that they eat only vegetables. They regard one day in the Jewish year better than another. They don't drink wine. The strong, on the other hand, understand their freedom in Jesus Christ who has declared all foods clean. Nothing is off limits. I can drink wine as long as I do not become drunk. I'm no longer bound to recognize and celebrate the special days of the Jewish year. And Paul counts himself among the strong. He says, "We who are strong have an obligation to bear the weaknesses of the weak."

Note that it's not "bear with" the failings of the weak. The word *with* has to be supplied in our English translations. If you think of "bearing with" somebody the way we usually think about that phrase, you're missing the gravity of Paul's point. To bear the weaknesses of those who are not strong doesn't simply mean to tolerate them. Rather, Paul is describing the community of faith created by Jesus Christ. Not everybody is going to be in the same place when it comes to their faith. Those who are stronger have an obligation, not just to tolerate their brothers and sisters who are weaker, but to carry those who are weak. They're not simply to endure the irritating things those who are weaker say and do.

The strong are strong not to please themselves, but to help sustain and support those who are weak in order to build up one another. By the time Paul's readers reached this point in his letter, he had already set them up for this implication of their lives as Christians back in 5:6-8: "For while we were still weak, at the right time Christ died for the ungodly. For one will scarcely die for a righteous person—though perhaps for a good person one would dare even to die—but God shows his love for us in that while we were still sinners, Christ died for us." While explaining the gospel, Paul said Jesus Christ, the strongest one, gave his life for the weak ones—us. Christ has already done the bearing of the weak, and he didn't simply bear with our weakness; he carried it in his body on the cross. You see, what Paul is talking about is the cruciform aspect of the Christian community—the cross-formed cost-counting aspect.

Our freedom in Christian community is much more than the freedom to eat what we want and to drink what we want. Our freedom is the freedom to lay down our lives for our brothers and sisters. Our liberty as Christians is the liberty to die to our own preferences, the liberty to die to our disordered desire to please ourselves all the time. Our freedom as Christians is the freedom to say to our neighbors, "We want to see you grow to maturity in Christ. Our heart's desire is to do every-thing we can to edify you, to build you up in the faith, to see you come to maturity in Christ." And this is something that we are to pursue, building each other up, edifying one another, pleasing one another.

We're not left to figure out what this looks like. Paul says that even Christ "did not please himself, but as it is written, 'The insults of those who insulted you have fallen on me.' (Putting the words of Psalm 69:9 in the mouth of Jesus Christ.) For whatever was written beforehand was written for our instruction, so that through the endurance and encouragement of the Scriptures we might have hope" (vv. 3-4, author's translation). God intends the endurance and encouragement of the Scriptures to give us hope for the here and now for our life together as his people.

Endurance is a primary application point for us in counting the cost. So, *do not look for a quick fix!* If your church has been mono-ethnic, mono-cultural, mono-socioeconomic and you are convinced that the Lord is calling you out of that mono-ghetto, you cannot expect overnight change. It's going to take much more than one small group Bible study or a handful of sermon series on racial reconciliation. Change is difficult and long. There's a reason that long-suffering is a fruit of the Spirit (Galatians 5:22). Be prepared to embrace ongoing interaction with two practices that help create and sustain a beautiful community: confession and forgiveness and the proper exercise of power.

Confession and forgiveness. I love how Henri Nouwen expresses the liberation that takes place in confession. He calls confession a discipline by which true incarnation may be lived. Confession brings the dark powers out of their carnal isolation into the light making them visible to the community. Of course, connected to confession is repentance, the act of turning around and going in the opposite direction. The liberation that comes through confession is among the most painful of all liberations. However, the first difficult step of repentance takes one a good distance on the road to reconciliation.

In *The Anatomy of the Soul,* Dr. Curt Thompson says, "We are to be people who are as fully known by each other as possible. This is accomplished in the freedom and power of confession and forgiveness." Those practices help to create communities that are flexible, adaptive, coherent, energized, and stable. While neither confession nor forgiveness is easy, they are key practices for beautiful community because the injuries from our fractured ghettoized lives cannot be undone. Confession and forgiveness are the only way out if we want to live in a manner worthy of our calling, pursuing the unity of the Spirit in the bond of peace.

The exercise of power. We've already said that the dignity embedded in humanity is royal dignity because we are the image of God. And it includes a legitimate authority rooted in one's very being. This authority, which by necessity includes the exercise of power, was given to us before sin entered the picture and dominance became the norm. Andy Crouch asks whether "the deepest truth about the world is a struggle for mastery and domination, or collaboration, cooperation, and ultimately love." Our experiences in almost every facet of life say to us that power is to be exercised for dominance. The truth is that power at its best, or in its intended proper use, is meant for flourishing. The proper use of power in beautiful community assumes that people are authorized to exercise power transfigured by love. This is the point: power transfigured by love.

Korie Edwards expresses this challenge by describing her discovery that "in interracial churches, those who wield power affirm white privilege and culture. . . . Consequently, African Americans will bear the greater burden of maintaining a racially mixed worship experience." She is not claiming that this is the result of malicious intent. Rather, it is an implication of the way cultural values operate beneath the surface. So, we have to engage the way power is exercised.

Let me offer some recommendations for what counting the cost in this way may look like.

Counting the cost in majority-culture churches. If you have never served under minority leadership, find ways to put yourself in an accountable relationship where you are under the influence and counsel of a minority leader. You need to experience that situation for an extended period of time. It may look like hiring a mentor or coach or spending your sabbatical in a minority church, under minority leadership, and seeking to continue a formal relationship following that season.

If your congregation has little familiarity with minority leadership and the church is seeking to hire a minority pastor or other ministry leader, be mindful of a few things: First, if you have a predominately white staff, be aware of the potential trauma a minority leader will experience in your context. You may not be ready as a congregation to hire a minority leader! Part of knowing whether or not you are means asking whether or not you will vest this person with real authority. It can be disastrous for both the individual and the church to bring a minority on in a lower-level staff position where people do not really have to submit to their authority. Structural inclusion of people of color into influential positions is an aspect of the proper exercise of power and of hospitality. Christerson, Edwards, and Emerson found structural inclusion to be one of the ways leaders can move people away from the edge and toward the core of an interracial religious organization. But it has to be pursued with authenticity, not as a way of creating a statistical diversity within the church structures. Diverse churches must value people by making room for them in fellowship and worship. Leadership has the responsibility of exercising authority in a way that facilitates this kind of welcome and embrace.

Bringing someone on as an intern, for example, means that the person has little influence, but will likely bear a heavy load as the minority representative. Instead, hire someone for a position with decision making authority and when you do, take steps to determine where and how this person will find the necessary connections with people who share their culture and ethnicity. Similarity is important.

The need for the presence of ethnic and cultural similarity emerged in my research as a major theme among the ways people experience belonging in a diverse church. People need to see themselves represented either in the congregation or some aspect of leadership. This is particularly true for ethnic minority participants. Without the presence of similarity, the differences can become too overwhelming to bear. As committed as I am to the pursuit of beautiful community, I know that African Americans committed to the same pursuit still need to have connection with other African Americans for periods of time. Minorities will often feel the pressure of code switching and assimilating into majority culture norms. Sometimes they need spaces where they don't experience that pressure. As a practical matter, my wife and I periodically host a get-together for people of color who are striving to flourish in diverse churches in our area. This coming together for refreshment in a culturally comfortable context actually helps them to continue pursuing beautiful community.

Counting the cost in minority-culture churches. The particular challenge for minority churches stems from their having been the place of safety, affirmation, and health for minority communities in America. This is especially true for the Black church, which has consistently affirmed human dignity for African Americans. As we saw in the last chapter, it has always cared for the full person, faith, education, health care, employment, relationships, and so on. As such, introducing diversity creates a legitimate fear of losing that identity. Articulating this fear sounds like, "We will lose who we are because when white people come in, they're used to getting things their way, and will take over." At the same time, the blessing of minority churches pursuing unity in diversity at a congregation level is that majority culture folks can benefit from the minority experience. Neither the individual nor the congregation gets a pass from the imperative to pursue unity in diversity. The minority church has learned how to thrive as a marginalized minority with limited to no agency in the culture. What a great gift it has to offer!

Let's take the heritage of song in the Black church tradition, forged from incredible suffering, as an example. It's a body of songs expressing the reality of a tragic human condition and the hope of a future glory. In the early 1900s, James Weldon Johnson wrote the poem "O Black and Unknown Bards" as an ode to the composers and singers of the Negro Spirituals. It is a striking poem, and the questions posed in the third stanza are particularly poignant.

> What merely living clod, what captive thing
> Could up toward God through all its darkness grope,
> And find within its deadened heart to sing
> These songs of sorrow, love and faith, and hope?

He declares at the end of the poem that the singers sang a race from wood and stone to Jesus Christ. A lot has changed and improved since the 1900s, but the heritage is still a balm. Look for opportunities to bless majority-culture pastors seeking to lead the churches they serve toward a more faithful expression of the unity that we have in Christ. Don't do so in an arrogant way, but with a gift giving, stewardship attitude regarding the faithfulness of God toward your community.

Time and again churches ask me, "What do we need to do to become more diverse?" The answer to that question is always contextual and local. Counting the cost is an overarching need with details particular to the people, place, and time. In fact, we take people through a three-year curriculum to not only probe their preferences, but also to discern the cost of the pursuit for them. The changes they will need to implement must be deliberate and dispersed from the pulpit to the pew. The Spirit of Christ loves to empower us to move toward beautiful community. But rest assured, he will change us in the process. There is an unavoidable degree of dissonance, conflict, disharmony, tension, and discomfort that arises from cultivating a more beautiful community. It is not for the faint of heart.

10

OUR HOLY AND BEAUTIFUL HOUSE

Toast to the Truth

With her poem **"Wreck This Journal,"** spoken-word poet Mazaré seeks to capture the essence of racial reconciliation, both what it is and what it isn't. In one stanza she says,

This work is more hug than curtsy,

more embrace than hat tip.

But start there.

Toast to the truth that I am different and dazzling.

She is encouraging a celebratory and hopeful tone to the work of reconciliation. As image-bearers all people have inherent dignity. It is the church's responsibility to find ways to affirm the full humanity—the royal dignity—of all people, especially those whom others are inclined to despise. The impact of racial hierarchy, privilege, and class in society has a substantial impact on the way people interact with one another and value themselves. The church is not immune to this dynamic. It cannot simply be said, "Just believe in Jesus, and those cross-racial social challenges will disappear." You don't overcome the dignity dynamic simply by believing in Jesus together. When we devote to the doctrine, probe the preferences, and count the cost of pursuing this kingdom vision it will seem daunting—even depressing. However, there is joy in the pursuit as we toast to the truth of the beautiful diverse community that God desires to create.

Christine Pohl says that gratitude operates at "several different levels: thanksgiving and praise to God, gratitude as a posture for life, and gratitude as a response to others for who they are or for what they have given to us." She notes that as important as it is to the well-being of individuals, its importance as a practice for community life has mostly been overlooked. It is "vital to sustaining communities that are holy and good." Gratitude builds community while ingratitude destroys it.

It is the church's responsibility to find ways to affirm the full humanity—the royal dignity—of all people, especially those whom others are inclined to despise.

In Scripture, God's people are often referred to as saints or holy ones. With the exception of Jesus, the holy and righteous one, that identity marker doesn't describe sinlessness in the here and now. It describes our identity as those covered by the blood of Jesus. This is the identity of the diverse churches we find addressed in the New Testament epistles. Earlier, we saw the earth-shattering and identity-defining description of the diverse Colossian church as, "God's chosen ones, holy and beloved" (Colossians 3:12). This community of Greek, Jew, barbarian, Scythian, slave, and free was chosen, made holy, and loved by God together. The final chord I want to strike in the cultivation of beautiful community is the joy inherent in being a grateful people. As we pursue beautiful community, gratitude is the attitude that God wants to cultivate in us. Remember the three facets of beauty: perfection, proportion, and pleasure? We find this trifecta of gratitude and beauty in Colossians 3:15-17:

And let the peace of Christ rule in your hearts, to which indeed
you were called in one body. And be thankful. Let the word of
Christ dwell in you richly, teaching and admonishing one another in all wisdom, singing psalms and hymns and spiritual
songs, with thankfulness in your hearts to God. And whatever
you do, in word or deed, do everything in the name of the Lord
Jesus, giving thanks to God the Father through him.

Let's take a look at how those facets of beauty and the pursuit of beautiful community are portrayed for us in those three verses.

PROPORTION

When we say that proportion is an aspect of beauty, we are saying that
harmony matters. The mystery of proportion is the presence of unity
in diversity, meaning it points to shalom, peace as a facet of beautiful
community. So, when it comes to us, life is not simply about us as individuals. Again, God isn't just making a new *me*, he's making a new *we*.

Jesus Christ is our peace. He is our only hope for peace with God.
What that means is that in Jesus Christ we are restored to wholeness
and flourishing in our relationship with God. So, Paul says to this new
we, "And let the peace of Christ rule in your hearts, to which indeed
you were called in one body. And be thankful" (Colossians 3:15). The
command indicates that something must rule and the subject of that
command is not "you all," but the "peace of Christ." The term translated *rule* here has the sense of an arbitrator or umpire, like in baseball.
When tension and difficulty arise, what is the determining factor in
how you respond? What makes the call between balls and strikes in
your decisions? What is it that tells you, "Do this, not that," "Say this,
not that"? Is it your feelings? Are you driven by how you feel in the
moment? Is it your preferences?

Notice that the peace of Christ is something that the Colossians are
told to "let" happen, not "make" happen. Paul doesn't write, "Make the

peace of Christ rule." Rather, he instructs them to let the fact that they have been reconciled to peace with God reign as the ruling factor in their decision making.

You didn't call yourself into this life. God called you. God placed you in this one body. It's not even your body. It's the body of Christ. You've been called into peaceful existence in this body that God placed you in. Were it not for the blood of Jesus, you would have remained at a distance because of your differences and divisions. The pursuit that creates peace only happens when we live in a position of gratitude for that peace. When Paul writes, "And be thankful," it's not a throwaway line! He means, "Keep on being thankful." Continue expressing gratitude for the peace that Jesus Christ has made for you with God by the blood of his cross.

Dietrich Bonhoeffer hits the mark when he links the necessity of gratitude to the sustaining of Christian community. He strove to maintain faithful fellowship even while the German church was under pressure from the Nazi government to compromise its values. He exhorts,

> If we do not give thanks daily for the Christian fellowship in which we have been placed, even where there is no great experience, no discoverable riches, but much weakness, small faith, and difficulty; if on the contrary, we only keep complaining to God that everything is so paltry and petty, so far from what we expected, then we hinder God from letting our fellowship grow according to the measure and riches that are there for us all in Jesus Christ.

Our gratitude for the community is connected to our commitment to the community, even if the community is not extraordinary! When our differences manifest themselves in difficulty and tension, our attitude of gratitude is grounded in the peace we have with God and one another through Jesus Christ.

PERFECTION

In Colossians 3:14, the apostle points to love as the binding glue of perfection for this diverse church. Recall that when it comes to beauty, its perfection can still accommodate scars. In fact, it's a perfection that must accommodate scars. Paul says in verse 16, "Let the word of Christ dwell in you richly, teaching and admonishing one another in all wisdom." He means, "Let the word of Christ live in your hearts." Notice how he instructs them to do this—teaching and admonishing each other, singing psalms, hymns, and spiritual songs with gratitude to God. The word of Christ is God's declaration of who Jesus is, what he is doing, and why he is doing it. This is the word the Colossians are instructed to have living richly among them as they teach and warn each other. The community in Colossae, like ours today, faced the challenge of striving together in faithfulness to Jesus Christ, a difficult task because the stratifications in society do not tend toward unity and reconciliation for Greeks and Jews, slaves and free people. They bring their wounds with them into the community of Christ.

That's why Paul writes with intention here. Look at what he said to the Colossians in 1:28-29: "Him we proclaim, warning everyone and teaching everyone with all wisdom, that we may present everyone mature in Christ. For this I toil, struggling with all his energy that he powerfully works within me." Paul is talking about himself as an apostle, working hard to proclaim Christ, warning and teaching with all wisdom. His goal is their maturity in Christ. But when he gets to chapter 3, he says this isn't only his responsibility to his readers; it is also for the Colossians to do with and for one another. He uses the same words, "teaching and admonishing one another in all wisdom" (3:16). In other words, he is telling them to not only look to him as an apostle, but also to trust that as the peace of Christ rules in their hearts, as the word of Christ lives lavishly among them, God will grant wisdom so that they can grow in maturity together.

This dwelling of the word of Christ with wisdom while teaching and warning happens when we come together for worship. It happens when we sing psalms, hymns, and spiritual songs with gratitude in our hearts to God. Isn't it wonderful that Paul calls out corporate singing in particular as a way we let the word of Christ live richly in us—as a way we teach and warn one another? What do think when you gather corporately and sing? Do you picture you and God on an island alone? Do you ever think about the people of God in your praise?

Every church member I spoke with in my research expressed this aspect of gratitude as they began to forge authentic friendships in their church. For Eun the experience of gratitude grew when she believed the people around were genuinely listening and "trying to be as real as possible." She described this authenticity as knowing that "People are not being nice for the sake of being nice 'cause you're a Christian."

The lack of perceived authenticity at All Saints hindered Joyce from experiencing belonging in her first three years at the church. As mentioned in chapter 1, she was asked to serve on a ministry board shortly after joining the church. The request hindered her experience of belonging because she felt it was not authentic. She had just started attending the church. The combination of their request with the fact that they did not know much about her led her to believe that they were inauthentic. Thankfully, she stayed long enough for that perception to begin to change. The shift took place at the church's women's retreat when some non-Black women she believed to be inauthentic opened up to her. Their vulnerability made her willing to open up to them. She began to experience them as family with a vital sense of connection. Deep friendships were able to develop.

Authentic friendships developed through a willingness to be vulnerable with Dinesh as well. Some cultural differences at Christ the King Church manifested themselves in communication challenges between people. Even so, he found a sense of belonging with people who were not afraid to be vulnerable and with whom he felt he could be vulnerable. As a result, he has developed close relationships across ethnic lines in the church and has been willing to initiate this kind of vulnerability. "I can share my thoughts before them; my struggles before them." He has learned to be someone willing to take the risk of sharing his deep struggles. Embracing vulnerability and developing authentic friendships has happened for him even as he's wondered whether he should stay at the church. "In the midst of this struggle," he said, "I find that I belong there. That's the work of the Spirit."

Andrea said that part of the blessing in being a member of a diverse church is being pushed out of cultural comforts. It keeps you "on the hook" to engage relationally with others who are different and have diverse perspectives. She explained,

> What happens over time is you don't feel like you're the only one having to engage. It starts to be reciprocated. You get challenged on a couple of things, but you've created a relationship enough that you know that person. You trust their motive, and you work on that together. That takes time. It takes, I think, humility, and it takes really resting on Christ to do that.

Mark McMinn helpfully posits that the goal is not just to enable close relationships, but healing relationships. Relationships outside of a relationship with God "sometimes disappoint and devastate and evoke our self-sufficiency and sinfulness in ways that are far from healthy. Many close relationships do more damage than good." He explains that it is necessary to consider the interaction between self, brokenness, and healing relationships for a comprehensive perspective on psychological and spiritual health. Authentic friendships are akin to healing relationships that allow people to experience grace and hope in the middle of life's trials. This healing happened in these churches as people embraced vulnerability and decided to trust across racial and ethnic lines.

PLEASURE

Finally, we rejoice because beauty delights. Paul expands the attitude of gratitude to the entirety of our lives. "And whatever you do, in word or deed, do everything in the name of the Lord Jesus, giving thanks to God the Father through him" (Colossians 3:17). In practice, the attitude of gratitude in practice is meant to spill out of Sunday worship into a joyful everyday living. There is a delight in a daily practice of gratitude to God for the fact that we are dazzling and different. I have not at any point in this book glossed over the difficulty of living into beautiful community. And I will not do so now, even as I talk about delight. Remember that God wants us to know him and this knowledge of him is for our delight! The delight of beauty is a de-centered delight in another—God himself.

We can give thanks to God in everything at all times by believing that he wastes nothing. In Revelation 21:4 the apostle John hears a loud voice from heaven tell him that God will wipe away every tear and remove death, mourning, crying, and pain. Those things will one day pass away, but please know that today's tears, deaths, mourning, crying, and pains are not wasted. In the context of Revelation, John is focused on persecution, tribulation, and suffering that Christians must persevere through. He's setting before them a vision of their glorious future, straining for adequate language to describe the beauty of Jesus' bride once she is fully healed from her ghettoized and painful existence (Revelation 22:2). At the same time, the pain in our pursuit of beautiful community will be healed as well! This promise allows us to delight in the here and now. Our tears and pain are not wanted, but they're not wasted either!

We can give thanks to God in everything at all times by believing that he wastes nothing.

What John sees in Revelation 21:2 is the holy city descending out of heaven from God after being prepared and adorned for her husband. These are passive verbs. The emphasis is on God who prepares and adorns his bride. He selects the wedding dress, styles the makeup and hair—he even drives the limo because the text tells us that his bride came down *from* God! How did he prepare her for the wedding day? Through tears, mourning, crying, and pain. He equipped her to endure by faith as a part of her beautification.

FOOD, GLORIOUS FOOD

I want to end with pleasure, the third part of beauty's triplet, because the tone is set at the table. Toasting to the truth paints a picture in our mind's eye of raising a glass at the dinner table. It never ceases to amaze me how replete the Bible is with food from beginning to end. Food is a good gift from God, and eating is not only nourishing, it's also delightful. Just like things are more beautiful than they need to be, food is more pleasurable than it needs to be. We have to eat to live, but God is so wonderful that he blesses food for our enjoyment. That enjoyment, in turn, should move us to bless God. Paul writes, "So, whether you eat or drink, or whatever you do, do all to the glory of God" (1 Corinthians 10:31).

The picture of God's covenant commitment to his people regularly involves food. When the Lord confirms his covenant with his people, calling Moses, Aaron, Nadab, Abihu, and seventy elders of Israel up to Mount Sinai, Exodus 24 tells us, "They saw the God of Israel. There was under his feet as it were a pavement of sapphire stone, like the very heaven for clearness. And he did not lay his hand on the chief men of the people of Israel; they beheld God, and ate and drank" (vv. 10-11). When the Lord promises the redemption that will put death to death and wipe away tears from all faces, he wants us to picture a wonderful feast. "On this mountain the LORD of hosts will make for all peoples a feast of rich food, a feast of well-aged wine, of rich food full of marrow, of aged wine well refined" (Isaiah 25:6). John envisions the blessing of the new heavens and earth as a wedding reception: "And the angel said to me, 'Write this: Blessed are those who are invited to the marriage supper of the Lamb.' And he said to me, 'These are the true words of God'" (Revelation 19:9). We could go on and on about the provision of abundant grain in the Old Testament, Jesus turning water into wine, the saints of the New Testament churches providing resources for famine relief of the church in Jerusalem, but it's clear that food is inseparable from beautiful community.

So, it came as no surprise that participants in my research regularly brought up eating together as an aspect of the way they experience belonging in their diverse church. In most instances the meals were crosscultural experiences. Who do you invite to your table? There is a reason Christians use the phrase *table fellowship* to describe eating together.

Do you want to rejoice in the pursuit of beautiful community? Come to the table and eat, the one that belongs to the Lord. What do we experience at the Lord's Supper? How do you think about communion? Do you see it as merely a personal, individual act, grateful for the fact that you get to participate because of Jesus? That's true, but are you able to see that it's much more than that? I want to invite you to experience the Lord's Supper as a multinational, diverse, ethnicity-affirming meal that is preparing us for the international wedding supper of the Lamb. The table keeps getting longer and more diverse as the Lord continues to add seats by redeeming people from every nation, from all tribes and peoples and languages.

Can you picture the nations coming to the feast with joy? Some approaching with moccasins on their feet, others dressed in Kente, or saris, or overalls, still others with turbans on their heads! And the one raising the glass for the toast is the bridegroom! He speaks and reminds us of how he told the disciples at the Last Supper that he would not drink again of the fruit of the vine until that day when he drank it new with them in his Father's kingdom (Matthew 26:29).

That new day has fully arrived! And as he raises the glass he's not looking up in the sky. Rather he's looking everyone in the eye with a loving gaze that communicates, "I see you. I made you. I redeemed you. You're welcomed at my table as queens and kings, a kingdom of priests."

Following Jesus' lead enables us to keep our eyes open and live for beauty right now. Doing so enables us to actively resist the pernicious polarization that has been present in the church in America from the beginning. We celebrate the fact that the triune God—Father, Son, and Holy Spirit—who exists in eternal beauty and glory, refused to turn his eyes away from the darkness of the world. So, the Son left his beautiful communion to take on our fragility, weakness, and vulnerability so that he could restore us to communion with God and each other. And our great joy is that in our pursuit of beautiful community, we are participating in the beautiful plan and purpose of our beautiful God.

ACKNOWLEDGMENTS

I **am enveloped in love.** As I write this, my wife, Kim, and I are closing in on twenty-eight years of marriage. We have been together on many peaks and in many valleys, and she has loved me through it all. This book would not have happened without her patience, support, and encouragement. Not only that, but the love of our four incredible children, Jelani, Nabil, Zakiya, and Jeremiah, has buoyed me. They fill my heart with gladness.

I am immeasurably indebted to my parents, Irwyn and Margaret, for forming me with an identity of dignity. Although Dad has gone on to glory and Mom is beset with dementia, their voices still speak loudly. And what a gift it is that my younger sister, Leslie, is not only blood, but also my close friend.

I extend deep gratitude to the men and women who shared their stories with me and answered my questions so vulnerably and willingly. I cannot tell you how privileged I feel to have been entrusted with them.

My theological instruction at Reformed Theological Seminary in Washington, DC helped give me biblical and theological language for my ministry passion, most particularly through the instruction of my professor, mentor, and friend, the late Reverend Dr. Howard Griffith. You don't meet many men like him in life.

As I dug deeper into pastoral ministry, pursuing beautiful community in practice, four Covenant Theological Seminary faculty helped sharpen me through the doctor of ministry degree. Drs. Bruce McRae and Phil Douglass are gold. Dr. Tasha Chapman is a rare jewel. Words cannot express how grateful I am to Dr. Mark Pfuetze for his guidance through my dissertation.

A special, special thank you goes to the leaders and members of the two churches I have been blessed to serve in pastoral ministry: City of Hope Presbyterian Church, in Columbia, Maryland, and Grace Presbyterian Church of Washington, DC.

Perhaps the greatest debt of gratitude I owe for my pastoral formation is to the Reverend Kevin Smith (aka Rev. Kev). I came under his pastorate as a much younger man, needing to see and learn from a faithful undershepherd. He was, and is, that for me. His love for Christ and Christ's church, bearing the burdens and sorrows of the flock, and his rejoicing in their blessings left an indelible mark on the way I strive to pastor others.

Without question, every glory goes to our triune God. Glory be to the Father and to the Son and to the Holy Spirit! My prayer is that this book will be a blessing to his church as more image-bearers are brought to embrace the loving unity in diversity, the beautiful community that reflects his inner life.

NOTES

FOREWORD BY TIMOTHY KELLER

3   *Translocal and transethnic*: Larry Hurtado, *Destroyer of the Gods: Early Christian Distinctiveness in the Roman World*, (Waco, Texas: Baylor University Press, 2016), 92-93.

INTRODUCTION

6   *Stamped from the beginning*: See Ibram Kendi's book *Stamped from the Beginning: The Definitive History of Racist Ideas in America* (New York: Nations Books, 2016).

6   *In my life*: I have also explored this topic in my essay for "The Witness," www.thewitnessbbc.com/afrocentricity-church.

7   *Yosef A.A. ben-Jochannan*: For some other influential books authored by Dr. Ben, as he was fondly called, consider reading *Our Black Seminarians and Black Clergy Without a Black Theology, The Need for a Black Bible*, and *Black Man of the Nile and His Family*.

7   *The idea of Afrocentricity*: It ought to be noted that he did publish another, earlier work, *Afrocentricity: The Theory of Social Change* (Buffalo: Amulefi, 1980). However, the books mentioned above were, in my experience, more central to defining the Afrocentric worldview.

7   *Christianity makes us submit*: Perhaps unknowingly, Asante stated something that is biblically accurate for all peoples. Paul told the Galatians that before they knew God, they were enslaved to those that were by nature not gods (Gal 4:8). The God of the Bible is strange, and a stranger, to everyone who is not in Christ.

7   *It needed to realize*: Molefi K. Asante, *Afrocentricity* (Trenton, NJ: Africa World Press Inc., 1988), 71.

7   *Authentic contact to African religious expression*: Asante, *Afrocentricity*, 74-75.

7   *The Black church will then*: Asante, *Afrocentricity*, 77. Italics are mine.

8   *In the concluding words*: Martin Luther King Jr. "Where Do We Go from Here?" speech delivered at the eleventh-annual SCLC Convention, Atlanta, GA, August 16, 1967.

10   *The good news*: Peter Leithart, "On Why We Should Care About Church Unity," *Mars Hill Audio Journal* 136, (November 2017), https://marshillaudio.org/catalog/volume-136.

10 *To [Jesus] the kingdom exists*: Geerhardus Vos, *The Teaching of Jesus Concerning the Kingdom of God and the Church* (Grand Rapids, MI: Eerdmans, 1958), 50.

11 *We should think about*: John M. Frame, *The Doctrine of God (A Theology of Lordship)* (Phillipsburg, NJ: P&R Publishing, 2002), 390.

12 *Dutch Reformed theologian*: Herman Bavinck, *Reformed Dogmatics*, ed. John Bolt, trans. John Vriend, vol. 2, *God and Creation* (Grand Rapids, MI: Baker Academic, 2004), 254.

12 *Bavinck again says*: Bavinck, *Reformed Dogmatics*, 2:331.

1. THE HOLY AND BEAUTIFUL HABITATION *(Our Relational God)*

18 *As Charles Taylor writes*: Charles Taylor, *Sources of the Self: The Making of the Modern Identity* (Cambridge, MA: Harvard University Press, 1989), 15.

19 *Esther Lightcap Meek notes*: Esther Lightcap Meek, *Loving to Know: Covenant Epistemology* (Eugene, OR: Cascade Books, 2011), 37, Kindle.

19 *It wasn't a fact*: Meek, *Loving to Know*, 37.

19 *Rather than taking*: John M. Frame, *Systematic Theology: An Introduction to Christian Belief* (Phillipsburg, NJ: P&R Publishing, 2013), 37.

20 *It has always been*: Meek, *Loving to Know*, 36.

20 *Alec Motyer describes this verse*: J. A. Motyer, *The Prophecy of Isaiah: An Introduction & Commentary* (Downers Grove, IL: InterVarsity Press, 1996), 516.

21 *Professor and theologian*: John M. Frame, *The Doctrine of the Christian Life (A Theology of Lordship)* (Phillipsburg, NJ: P&R Publishing, 2008), 402.

25 *His is the face*: Meek, *Loving to Know*, 306.

2. THE BEAUTY OF THE LORD *(Our God Is Beautiful Community)*

27 *A dozen camels*: Laurel Wamsley, "A Dozen Camels Disqualified from Saudi Beauty Pageant over Botox Injections," NPR, January 24, 2018, www.npr.org/sections/thetwo-way/2018/01/24/580228837/a-dozen-camels-disqualified-from-saudi-beauty-pageant-over-botox-injections.

28 *Jonathan King rightly says*: Jonathan King, *The Beauty of the Lord: Theology as Aesthetics*, Studies in Historical and Systematic Theology (Bellingham, WA: Lexham Press, 2018), chap. 1, Kindle.

29 *Species or beauty*: Thomas Aquinas, *Summa Theologica*, trans. Fathers of the English Dominican Province, STh., I q.39 a.8 ad 1 (London: Burns, Oates, and Washbourne, n.d.).

29 *But the perfection*: Steven R. Guthrie, *Creator Spirit: The Holy Spirit and the Art of Becoming Human* (Grand Rapids, MI: Baker Academic, 2011), 199, Kindle.

29 *These marks*: Guthrie, *Creator Spirit*, 196.

30 *When all things*: Guthrie, *Creator Spirit*, 204.

31   *Beauty says*: Esther Lightcap Meek, *Loving to Know: Covenant Epistemology* (Eugene, OR: Cascade Books, 2011), 299, Kindle.

31   *If I were to ask*: Saint Augustine, cited in Umberto Eco, "The Function and Nature of the Aesthetic *Visio*," in *The Aesthetics of Thomas Aquinas*, trans. Hugh Bredin (Cambridge, MA: Harvard University Press, 1988), 49.

31   *Jonathan King refers*: King, *The Beauty of the Lord*, chap. 1, Kindle.

32   *Rather than drawing*: Guthrie, *Creator Spirit*, 207.

34   *None of his attributes*: John M. Frame, *The Doctrine of God (A Theology of Lordship)* (Phillipsburg, NJ: P&R Publishing, 2002), 226.

35   *God's character is whole*: Scott Redd, *The Wholeness Imperative: How Christ Unifies Our Desires, Identity and Impact in the World* (Ross-shire, Scotland: Christian Focus Publications, 2018), 20.

35   *The testimony throughout Scripture*: Frame, *The Doctrine of God*, 619-21.

37   *Far from a dry*: Herman Bavinck, *Reformed Dogmatics*, ed. John Bolt, trans. John Vriend, vol. 2, *God and Creation* (Grand Rapids, MI: Baker Academic, 2004), 288.

37   *Theologian Herman Bavinck says*: Bavinck, *Reformed Dogmatics*, 2:331.

38   *The Trinity belongs*: Gerald Bray, *The Doctrine of God* (Downers Grove, IL: InterVarsity Press, 1993), 119.

38   *The Father, Son, and Holy Spirit*: Stephen R. Holmes, *The Quest for the Trinity: The Doctrine of God in Scripture, History and Modernity* (Downers Grove, IL: InterVarsity Press, 2012), 21-22.

39   *The concurrence of*: Frame, *The Doctrine of God*, 694-95.

3. THE PERFECTION OF BEAUTY *(Knowing Ourselves)*

41   *Beauty brings copies*: Elaine Scarry, *On Beauty and Being Just* (Princeton, NJ: Princeton University Press, 1999), 3.

42   *Pratt goes so far*: Richard L. Pratt Jr., *Designed for Dignity: What God Has Made It Possible for You to Be* (Phillipsburg, NJ: P&R Publishing, 2000), 7, 17.

42   *The word*: Nonna Verna Harrison, *God's Many-Splendored Image: Theological Anthropology for Christian Formation* (Grand Rapids, MI: Baker Publishing Group), 90-91.

46   *John Frame*: John M. Frame, *The Doctrine of the Christian Life (A Theology of Lordship)* (Phillipsburg, NJ: P&R Publishing, 2008), 461.

46   *G. K. Beale*: G. K. Beale, *We Become What We Worship: A Biblical Theology of Idolatry* (Downers Grove, IL: IVP Academic, 2008), 276.

47   *Throughout the majority of my career*: excerpt from Sterling K. Brown's acceptance speech for the 2018 Golden Globe award, Best Actor in a TV Series, Drama, January 7, 2018, www.youtube.com/watch?v=4kGJTWzPABA.

48   *We are all born*: Curt Thompson, *The Soul of Shame: Retelling the Stories We Believe About Ourselves* (Downers Grove, IL: InterVarsity Press, 2015), 138.

48 *What is central*: Daphna Oyserman, Kristen Elmore, and George Smith, "Self, Self-Concept, and Identity," in *Handbook of Self and Identity*, ed. Mark R. Leary and June Prince Tangney (New York: The Guilford Press, 2012), 76.

48 *In his book*: Charles Taylor, *Sources of the Self: The Making of the Modern Identity* (Cambridge, MA: Harvard University Press, 1989), 15.

49 *I believe that Taylor*: Taylor, *Sources of the Self*, 15.

49 *Thus, a lack of knowledge*: Pratt, *Designed for Dignity*, 3.

49 *Failing to realize*: Pratt, *Designed for Dignity*, 21.

49 *The goal is*: R.C. Sproul, *Truths We Confess: A Layman's Guide to the Westminster Confession of Faith*, vol. 3, *The State, The Family, The Church, and Last Things* (Phillipsburg, NJ: P&R Publishing, 2006), 63.

49 *How do we know*: Steven R. Guthrie, *Creator Spirit: The Holy Spirit and the Art of Becoming Human* (Grand Rapids, MI: Baker Academic, 2011), 166, Kindle.

50 *The Christian view*: Kelly M. Kapic, Tim Morris, and Matthew S. Vos, "Where Does Authority Come from?: A Conversation with a Theologian, a Biologist, and a Sociologist," *Modern Reformation* 24, no. 5 (August 2015), www.whitehorseinn.org/issue/who-am-i.

50 *The image of God*: We see this sharpened countercultural message about the nature of the *imago Dei* in passages like 1 Corinthians 12:13, Galatians 3:28, Ephesians 4:15-22, Colossians 3:11, and Revelation 7:9.

50 *The whole concept*: Martin Luther King Jr., "The American Dream," preached at Ebenezer Baptist Church, Atlanta, GA, July 4, 1965.

51 *Memphis public works*: DeNeen L Brown, "'I Am a Man': The Ugly Memphis Sanitation Workers' Strike That Led to MLK's Assassination," *Washington Post*, February 12, 2018, www.washingtonpost.com/news/retropolis/wp /2018/02/12/i-am-a-man-the-1968-memphis-sanitation-workers-strike-that -led-to-mlks-assassination.

4. A CROWN OF BEAUTY IN THE HAND OF THE LORD
(Beautiful Community as God's Image)

53 *And you're*: Afua Hirsch, "Our identity | Afua Hirsch | TEDxTottenham," TEDx Talks, January 6, 2015, YouTube video, www.youtube.com/watch?v =TzhCpv9ynrM.

54 *God apparently loves difference*: Duane Elmer, *Cross Cultural Connections: Stepping Out and Fitting In Around the World* (Downers Grove, IL: InterVarsity Press, 2002), 64.

54 *There're not three*: Hirsch, "Our Identity."

54 *Connection is why*: Brené Brown, *Daring Greatly: How the Courage to Be Vulnerable Transforms the Way We Live, Love, Parent, and Lead* (New York: Gotham Books, 2012), page 8, Kindle.

54   *We are born*: Herman Bavinck, *Reformed Dogmatics*, ed. John Bolt, trans. John Vriend, vol. 4, *Holy Spirit, Church, and New Creation* (Grand Rapids, MI: Baker Academic, 2008), 276.

55   *Thine eye diffused*: Charles Wesley, "And Can It Be, That I Should Gain?" 1738.

55   *The image of God*: Herman Bavinck, *Reformed Dogmatics*, ed., John Bolt, trans. John Vriend, vol. 2, *God and Creation* (Grand Rapids, MI: Baker Academic, 2004), 577. An important point to note here is that Bavinck is focused on human destiny in community. The Scriptures tell us that Jesus is the image of the invisible God, the firstborn over all creation (Col 1:15). All the fulness of God was pleased to dwell in him (Col 1:19). There is a sense in which we may say that the *imago Dei* is fully realized in Jesus Christ. At the same time, Jesus' redeeming work ushers in the reconciliation of all things to himself, making peace by the blood of his cross (Col 1:20). So, included in our being reconciled to him and to one another is our renewal in the image of our creator (Col 3:10). There's no renewal into the image apart from Christian community (Col 3:11-17).

57   *Ethnic identity feels*: Aaron Kuecker, "Ethnicity and Social Identity," in *T&T Clark Handbook to Social Identity in the New Testament*, ed. J. Brian Tucker and Coleman A. Baker (New York: Bloomsbury, 2014), location 1725 of 18010, Kindle.

64   *To be in his hand*: J. A. Motyer, *The Prophecy of Isaiah: An Introduction & Commentary* (Downers Grove, IL: InterVarsity Press, 1996), 506.

5. YOUR BEAUTIFUL CROWN HAS COME DOWN FROM YOUR HEAD
(Ghettoization of Humanity)

71   *It conveys*: Bruce K. Waltke and Cathi J. Fredricks, *Genesis: A Commentary* (Grand Rapids, MI: Zondervan, 2001), 178.

71   *In chapter thirteen, Lot*: In Genesis 25:6, Abraham sends the children he bore to Keturah eastward, away from Isaac. This conveys that they are outside of the covenantal blessing that belonged to Isaac. In Genesis 29:1 when Jacob comes to the "people of the east" it's an indication that he's come to people who weren't worshippers of the Lord.

72   *Like Jacob's staircase*: Waltke and Fredricks, *Genesis*, 179.

74   *God comes down in judgment*: I have also written on this topic at Irwyn Ince, "Reconciliation or Bust," *Reformation 21*, April 17, 2012, www.reformation21 .org/articles/reconciliation-or-bust.php.

75   *Ibram X. Kendi defines*: Ibram X. Kendi, *Stamped from the Beginning: The Definitive History of Racist Ideas in America* (New York: Nation Books, 2016), 5.

75   *He writes that*: Kendi, *Stamped from the Beginning*, 9.

75   *He points out that*: Kendi, *Stamped from the Beginning*, 9.

76   *To be clear*: Michael O. Emerson and Christian Smith, *Divided by Faith: Evangelical Religion and the Problem of Race in America* (Oxford: Oxford University Press, 2000), location 193 of 4546, Kindle.

76   *Race, claims Dr. Korie Edwards*: Korie L. Edwards, *The Elusive Dream: The Power of Race in Interracial Churches* (Oxford: Oxford University Press, 2008), location 83-91 of 2682, Kindle.

76   *People placed*: Edwards, *The Elusive Dream*, location 127 of 2682.

76   *As my brother*: While it's true that the concept of race, as a way of differentiating people on the basis of skin color and other physical characteristics for the purpose of exploitation and oppression, is a human social construct, the Bible does differentiate between people groups. The common New Testament word is *ethnos*. However, another Greek word, *genos*, is often translated into English as "race." It primarily refers to kind, nationality, or family; people connected by common language, geography, descent, or religion. Indeed, it is translated with various English words depending on context. The important difference is that it does not imply ontological value the way race in our vernacular does.

77   *The framework*: Emerson and Smith, *Divided by Faith*, locations 228-30 of 4546.

78   *A reference to Judges 12*: Elissa Yukiko Weichbrodt, "Fault Lines," *View*, Autumn 2018: 18, www.covenant.edu/view/2018autumn/fault_lines.

78   *Sometimes we believe that dignity*: Weichbrodt, "Fault Lines," 19.

80   *But this is the elephant*: I am also aware that even phrasing the conversation this way is a centering on whiteness. One area that is worth exploration and research is the pursuit of unity in diversity from churches that come out of the minority experience.

80   *White structural advantage*: Korie L. Edwards, *The Elusive Dream: The Power of Race in Interracial Churches* (Oxford: Oxford University Press, 2008), location 144 of 2682, Kindle.

80   *White normativity*: Edwards, *The Elusive Dream*, location 151 of 2682, Kindle.

80   *White transparency*: Edwards, *The Elusive Dream*, location 161 of 2682, Kindle.

81   *If you're a part of a minority culture*: Mark Lau Branson and Juan F. Martinez, *Churches, Cultures & Leadership: A Practical Theology of Congregations and Ethnicities* (Downers Grove, IL: IVP Academic, 2011), 112.

6. I WILL BEAUTIFY MY BEAUTIFUL HOUSE *(Identity and Formation)*

82   *To be warm and embracing*: Brad Christerson, Korie L. Edwards, and Michael O. Emerson, *Against All Odds: The Struggle for Racial Integration in Religious Organizations* (New York: NYU Press, 2005), 16.

82   *The importance of people*: Christerson, Edwards, and Emerson, *Against All Odds*, 151-52.

82   *In the last couple*: Campbell Robertson, "A Quiet Exodus: Why Black Worshipers Are Leaving White Evangelical Churches," *The New York Times*, March 9, 2018, www.nytimes.com/2018/03/09/us/blacks-evangelical-churches.html.

83   *Reassuring uneasy fellow worshipers*: Robertson, "A Quiet Exodus."

84   *Through the person and work*: Anthony Bradley, "The Great Commission Christianity Keeps Blacks Away From Evangelicalism," *Fathom*, March 11, 2019, www.fathommag.com/stories/the-great-commission-christianity-keeps-blacks-away-from-evangelicalism.

85   *Glory be to God*: Gerald Manly Hopkins, "Pied Beauty," *Poems and Prose* (New York: Penguin Classics, 1985), www.poetryfoundation.org/poems/44399/pied-beauty.

88   *Few things*: David A. Livermore, *Cultural Intelligence: Improving Your CQ to Engage Our Multicultural World*, ed. Chap Clark (Grand Rapids, MI: Baker Academic, 2009), 86.

88   *By implication*: Randy Woodley, *Living in Color: Embracing God's Passion for Ethnic Diversity* (Downers Grove, IL: InterVaristy Press, 2004), 66.

88   *The New Normal*: Much of this material is taken from my chapter, "Regaining What We've Lost: The First Century Church," in *All Are Welcome: Toward a Multi-Everything Church* (Oklahoma City: Storied Publishing, 2008).

89   *We are family*: We are clued in on the fact that the Lord's concern is a reunion and unity for the world in the text itself. These nations will be a blessing in the "midst of the earth." As Alec Motyer points out, "The true bearing of the oracles which have focused on Egypt is that Egypt is a 'case in point' of the Lord's purpose to unite the world in his worship." J. A. Motyer, *The Prophecy of Isaiah: An Introduction & Commentary* (Downers Grove, IL: InterVarsity Press, 1996), 169.

91   *While there was definitely*: J. Daniel Hays, *From Every People and Nation: A Biblical Theology of Race* (Downers Grove, IL: InterVarsity Press, 2003), 141-42.

91   *So while it may be simple*: Of course, I realize that a relatively easy counter argument to this point is that Paul seems to do just that! For example, in Ephesians 2:11-16, he clearly categorizes the Christians in the Ephesian churches as either having been Gentiles ("the uncircumcision") or Jews ("the circumcision") as their primary identity before faith in Christ. But Christ has killed the hostility and made both one. However, to be a Gentile means to belong to a people group that does not profess faith in the God of Israel. It does not mean that all Gentiles were a common people group, nationality, or culture.

91   *Migrations and invasions*: Hays, *From Every People and Nation*, 141.

92   *There would be one Lord*: Eph 4:5-6.

95   *Only humanity in its entirety*: Herman Bavinck, *Reformed Dogmatics*, ed. John Bolt, trans. John Vriend, vol. 2, *God and Creation* (Grand Rapids, MI: Baker Academic, 2004), 577. An important point to note here is that Bavinck is focused on human destiny in community. The Scriptures tell us that Jesus is the image of the invisible God, the firstborn over all creation (Col 1:15). All the fulness of God was pleased to dwell in him (Col 1:19). There is a sense in which we may say that the *imago Dei* is fully realized in Jesus Christ. At the same time, Jesus' redeeming work ushers in the reconciliation of all things to himself, making peace by the blood of his cross (Col 1:20). So, included in our being reconciled to him and to one another is our renewal in the image of our creator (Col 3:10). There's no renewal into the image apart from Christian community (Col 3:11-17).

96   *A powerful expression of*: Kuecker, "Ethnicity and Social Identity," in *T&T Clark Handbook to Social Identity in the New Testament*, ed. J. Brian Tucker and Coleman A. Baker (New York: Bloomsbury, 2014), location 1627 of 18010.

96   *While Israel saw itself*: *Ho Laos* means "the people" and *ethneae* means "Gentile."

96   *The Gentiles constituted*: Kuecker, "Ethnicity and Social Identity," location 1627 of 18010.

96   *As I mentioned*: Kuecker, "Ethnicity and Social Identity," location 1725 of 18010.

97   *[Because] members interpret*: Christerson, Edwards, and Emerson, *Against All Odds*, 33-34.

97   *Trapped within the claims*: Miroslav Volf, *Exclusion and Embrace: A Theological Exploration of Identity, Otherness, and Reconciliation* (Nashville: Abingdon Press, 1996), 37.

97   *God alone has the wisdom*: Dennis E. Johnson, *The Message of Acts in the History of Redemption* (Phillipsburg, NJ: P&R Publishing, 1997), 102.

97   *With the Holy Spirit*: Bruce K. Waltke and Cathi J. Fredricks, *Genesis: A Commentary* (Grand Rapids, MI: Zondervan, 2001), 184.

7. PUT ON YOUR BEAUTIFUL GARMENTS *(Culture and Community)*

99   *More expressly*: Peter Block, *Community: The Structure of Belonging* (San Francisco: Berrett-Koehler Publishers, 2008), xii.

101   *Remain racially integrated*: Korie L. Edwards, *The Elusive Dream: The Power of Race in Interracial Churches* (Oxford: Oxford University Press, 2008), locations 96 of 2682, Kindle.

101   *In order to understand*: Edwards, *The Elusive Dream*, locations 91-93 of 2682, Kindle.

106   *Values while honestly*: Presbyterian Church in America, *Minutes of the Thirty-Eighth General Assembly of the Presbyterian Church in America*

(Nashville: Presbyterian Church in America, 2010), 440, http://pcahistory.org/pca/ga/38th_pcaga_2010.pdf.

106 *The PCA identify*: Presbyterian Church in America, *Minutes*, 440.

107 *Maintaining biblical worship*: Presbyterian Church in America, *Minutes*, 13.

107 *Ethnic homogeneity*: Presbyterian Church in America, *Minutes*, 14.

107 *[W]e still have*: Jonathan Merritt, "Southern Baptist Convention: Can It Thrive in the 21st Century?" *Religion News Service*, June 9, 2014, https://religionnews.com/2014/06/09/southern-baptist-convention-acing-thrive-21st-century.

107 *We have to learn*: David A. Livermore, *Cultural Intelligence: Improving Your CQ to Engage Our Multicultural World*, ed. Chap Clark (Grand Rapids, MI: Baker Academic, 2009), 34.

108 *Westminster Confession of Faith*: WCF 26.1. All saints, that are united to Jesus Christ their Head, by His Spirit, and by faith, have fellowship with Him in His grace, sufferings, death, resurrection, and glory: and, being united to one another in love, they have communion in each other's gifts and graces, and are obliged to the performance of such duties, public and private, as do conduce to their mutual good, both in the inward and outward man.

108 WCF 26.2. Saints by profession are bound to maintain an holy fellowship and communion in the worship of God, and in performing such other spiritual services as tend to their mutual edification; as also in relieving each other in outward things, according to their several abilities and necessities. Which communion, as God offers opportunity, is to be extended unto all those who, in every place, call upon the name of the Lord Jesus.

108 WCF 26.3. This communion which the saints have with Christ, does not make them in any wise partakers of the substance of His Godhead; or to be equal with Christ in any respect: either of which to affirm is impious and blasphemous. Nor does their communion one with another, as saints, take away, or infringe the title or propriety which each man has in his goods and possessions.

108 *Our resources are spiritual*: I have written more on this topic at Irwyn Ince, "Work and Pastoral Care" in *Public Justice Review: Faith, Family, and the Future of Work*, vol. 9, no. 1, (2019), https://cpjustice.org/uploads/Irwyn_FINAL1.pdf.

108 *Christian unity and union*: Robert Letham, *The Westminster Assembly: Reading Its Theology in Historical Context* (Phillipsburg, NJ: P&R Publishing, 2009), 323.

109 *Ultimately this love*: Chad Van Dixhoorn, *Confessing the Faith: A Reader's Guide to the Westminster Confession of Faith* (Edinburgh, UK: The Banner of Truth, 2014), 352.

109   *R. C. Sproul, reflecting on the Confession*: R.C. Sproul, *Truths We Confess: A Layman's Guide to the Westminster Confession of Faith*, vol. 3, *The State, The Family, The Church, and Last Things* (Phillipsburg, NJ: P&R Publishing, 2006), 72.

109   *We must here be admonished*: William Perkins, Thomas Pickering, and Thomas Pierson, *The Workes of That Famous and Vvorthy Minister of Christ in the Uniuersitie of Cambridge, Mr. William Perkins* (London, 1616), 312.

109   *Rather, it is a love*: George S. Hendry, *The Westminster Confession for Today* (Atlanta: John Knox Press, 1960), 219.

109   *Among us unity exists*: Herman Bavinck, *Reformed Dogmatics*, ed. John Bolt, trans. John Vriend, vol. 2, *God and Creation* (Grand Rapids, MI: Baker Academic, 2004), 331.

8. HOW BEAUTIFUL ARE THE FEET *(Gospel Message—Devote to the Doctrine)*

113   *The good news is*: Peter Leithart, "On Why We Should Care About Church Unity," *Mars Hill Audio Journal* 136, (November 2017), https://marshillaudio .org/catalog/volume-136.

114   *Truncated Great Commission*: Anthony Bradley, "The Great Commission Christianity Keeps Blacks Away from Evangelicalism," *Fathom*, March 11, 2019, www.fathommag.com/stories/the-great-commission-christianity -keeps-blacks-away-from-evangelicalism.

115   *What is the moral law?*: *The Larger Catechism* (Ross-shire, Scotland: Christian Heritage, 2018), 95.

116   *But all superiors*: The Catechism here uses the language of *superior* and *inferior*. This is not an ontological declaration, but a way of describing people in and under authority. Today we use words like *boss, manager, official*, and *employee, staff, subordinate*, and *junior* to communicate the same dynamic.

116   *WLC question 129*: Q. 129. What is required of superiors towards their inferiors?

117   A. It is required of superiors, according to that power they receive from God, and that relation wherein they stand, to love, pray for, and bless their inferiors; to instruct, counsel, and admonish them; countenancing, commending, and rewarding such as do well; and discountenancing, reproving, and chastising such as do ill; protecting, and providing for them all things necessary for soul and body: and by grave, wise, holy, and exemplary carriage, to procure glory to God, honor to themselves, and so to preserve that authority which God hath put upon them.

Q. 130. What are the sins of superiors?

A. The sins of superiors are, besides the neglect of the duties required of them, and inordinate seeking of themselves, their own glory, ease, profit, or pleasure; commanding things unlawful, or not in the power of inferiors to perform; counseling, encouraging, or favoring them in that which is evil; dissuading, discouraging, or discountenancing them in that which is good; correcting them unduly; careless exposing, or leaving them to wrong, temptation, and danger; provoking them to wrath; or any way dishonoring themselves, or lessening their authority, by an unjust, indiscreet, rigorous, or remiss behavior.

117 *As for the state*: Johannes G. Vos, *The Westminster Larger Catechism: A Commentary*, ed. G. I. Williamson (Phillipsburg, NJ: P&R Publishing, 2002), 351.

118 *You shall not murder*: Q. 135. What are the duties required in the sixth commandment?

A. The duties required in the sixth commandment are all careful studies, and lawful endeavors, to preserve the life of ourselves and others by resisting all thoughts and purposes, subduing all passions, and avoiding all occasions, temptations, and practices, which tend to the unjust taking away the life of any; by just defense thereof against violence, patient bearing of the hand of God, quietness of mind, cheerfulness of spirit; a sober use of meat, drink, physic, sleep, labor, and recreations; by charitable thoughts, love, compassion, meekness, gentleness, kindness; peaceable, mild and courteous speeches and behavior; forbearance, readiness to be reconciled, patient bearing and forgiving of injuries, and requiting good for evil; comforting and succoring the distressed and protecting and defending the innocent.

Q. 136. What are the sins forbidden in the sixth commandment?

The sins forbidden in the sixth commandment are, all taking away the life of ourselves, or of others, except in case of public justice, lawful war, or necessary defense; the neglecting or withdrawing the lawful and necessary means of preservation of life; sinful anger, hatred, envy, desire of revenge; all excessive passions, distracting cares; immoderate use of meat, drink, labor, and recreations; provoking words, oppression, quarreling, striking, wounding, and whatsoever else tends to the destruction of the life of any.

119 *The purport of this commandment*: John Calvin, *Institutes of the Christian Religion*, ed. Henry Beveridge, book 2, vol. 1 (Edinburgh: The Calvin Translation Society, 1845), 470.

120 *First black man*: David E. Swift, *Black Prophets of Justice: Activist Clergy Before the Civil War* (Baton Rouge: Louisiana State University Press, 1989), 19.

120 *In 1880 Pastor Matthew Anderson*: Matthew Anderson, *Presbyterianism: Its Relation to the Negro* (Philadelphia, PA: John McGill White & Co., 1897), 20.

120 *The apathy of*: Anderson, *Presbyterianism*, 28-29.

121   *I have always been ready:* Carter G. Woodson, ed., *The Works of Francis J. Grimké,* vol. 3, *Stray Thoughts and Meditations* (Washington, DC: The Associated Publishers Inc., 1942), 33.

9. THE BEAUTY OF HOLINESS *(Probe the Preferences and Count the Cost)*

123   *Many Washington neighborhoods:* Ted Mellnik and Carol Morello, "Washington: A World Apart," *The Washington Post,* November 9, 2013, www.washingtonpost.com/sf/local/2013/11/09/washington-a-world-apart.

124   *More and more families:* Robert D. Putnam, *Our Kids: The American Dream in Crisis* (New York: Simon & Schuster, 2015), 38.

124   *At one time:* Putnam, *Our Kids,* 22.

124   *Almost uninterruptedly:* Putnam, *Our Kids,* 22.

124   *An uneasy tension:* Glenn E. Bracey and Wendy Leo Moore, "'Race Tests': Racial Boundary Maintenance in White Evangelical Churches," *Sociological Inquiry* 87, no. 2 (April, 2017): 282.

124   *Members of an in-group:* Gordon W. Allport, *The Nature of Prejudice,* 25th anniversary ed. (Reading, MA: Addison-Wesley Pub. Co., 1979), 31.

125   *Because the familiar:* Allport, *The Nature of Prejudice,* 46.

125   *As a result:* Michael O. Emerson and Christian Smith, *Divided by Faith: Evangelical Religion and the Problem of Race in America* (Oxford: Oxford University Press, 2000), 10, Kindle.

125   *The shaping and transforming effect:* Soong-Chan Rah, *Many Colors: Cultural Intelligence for a Changing Church* (Chicago: Moody Publishers, 2010), locations 238-241 of 2811, Kindle.

125   *If we're going to love:* David A. Livermore, *Cultural Intelligence: Improving Your CQ to Engage Our Multicultural World,* ed. Chap Clark (Grand Rapids, MI: Baker Academic, 2009), 12.

125   *Individuals form connections:* Robert D. Putnam, *Bowling Alone: The Collapse and Revival of American Community* (New York: Simon & Schuster Paperbacks, 2000), 20.

127   *A newcomer to a church:* Rah, *Many Colors,* location 1136 of 2811.

127   *What type of hospitality:* Rah, *Many Colors,* location 2278 of 2811.

127   *Hospitable communities recognize:* Christine D. Pohl, *Living into Community: Cultivating Practices That Sustain Us* (Cambridge: Wm. B. Eerdmans Publishing Co., 2012), location 1913 of 2630, Kindle.

127   *Research shows:* Brad Christerson, Korie L. Edwards, and Michael O. Emerson, *Against All Odds: The Struggle for Racial Integration in Religious Organizations* (New York: NYU Press, 2005), 151-52.

127   *Core members from edge members:* Christerson, Edwards, and Emerson, *Against All Odds,* 154.

128   *In Miroslav Volf's view*: Miroslav Volf, *Exclusion and Embrace: A Theological Exploration of Identity, Otherness, and Reconciliation* (Nashville: Abingdon Press, 1996), 129.

128   *Our capacities*: Mark Lau Branson and Juan F. Martinez, *Churches, Cultures & Leadership: A Practical Theology of Congregations and Ethnicities* (Downers Grove, IL: IVP Academic, 2011), 112.

136   *Confession brings the dark*: Henri J. M. Nouwen, *In the Name of Jesus: Reflections on Christian Leadership* (New York: The Crossroad Publishing Company, 1989), 68.

136   *However, the first*: Volf, *Exclusion and Embrace*, 120.

136   *We are to be people*: Curt Thompson, *Anatomy of the Soul: Surprising Connections Between Neuroscience and Spiritual Practices That Can Transform Your Life and Relationships* (Carol Stream, IL: Tyndale, 2010), 249.

136   *Those practices*: Thompson, *Anatomy of the Soul*, 233.

137   *Royal dignity*: Nonna Verna Harrison, *God's Many-Splendored Image: Theological Anthropology for Christian Formation* (Grand Rapids, MI: Baker, 2010), 90.

137   *The deepest truth about the world*: Andy Crouch, *Playing God: Redeeming the Gift of Power* (Downers Grove, IL: InterVarsity Press, 2013), location 664 of 4947, Kindle.

137   *The truth is that power at its best*: Crouch, *Playing God*, location 450 of 4947.

137   *In interracial churches*: Korie L. Edwards, *The Elusive Dream: The Power of Race in Interracial Churches* (Oxford: Oxford University Press, 2008), location 485 of 2682, Kindle.

138   *Structural inclusion*: Christerson, Edwards, and Emerson, *Against All Odds*, 154.

140   *O Black and Unknown Bards*: James Weldon Johnson, "O Black And Unknown Bards," *The Books of the American Negro Spirituals*, ed. J. Rosamond Johnson (Boston: Da Capo Press, 1969; repr., New York: Viking Press, 1925, 1926), 11-12.

10. OUR HOLY AND BEAUTIFUL HOUSE *(Toast to the Truth)*

141   *It is the church's responsibility*: Nonna Verna Harrison, *God's Many-Splendored Image: Theological Anthropology for Christian Formation* (Grand Rapids, MI: Baker Publishing Group), 106.

141   *Just believe in Jesus*: Brad Christerson, Korie L. Edwards, and Michael O. Emerson, *Against All Odds: The Struggle for Racial Integration in Religious Organizations* (New York: NYU Press, 2005), 156.

142   *Several different levels*: Christine D. Pohl, *Living into Community: Cultivating Practices That Sustain Us* (Cambridge: Eerdmans, 2012), location 198 of 2630.

142   *Vital to sustaining*: Pohl, *Living into Community*, location 202 of 2630.

144   *If we do not give thanks*: Dietrich Bonhoeffer, *Life Together* (New York: Harper, 1954), 29.

147   *Sometimes disappoint*: Mark R. McMinn, *Psychology, Theology, and Spirituality in Christian Counseling*, rev. ed. (Wheaton, IL: Tyndale House, 2011; repr., Wheaton, IL: Tyndale House, 1996), 48.

147   *Authentic friendships*: McMinn, *Psychology, Theology, and Spirituality in Christian Counseling*, 51.